Also by Marcos Giralt Torrente

The End of Love

Father and Son

Father and Son

A Lifetime

Marcos Giralt Torrente

Translated from the Spanish by Natasha Wimmer

Sarah Crichton Books   Farrar, Straus and Giroux   New York

Sarah Crichton Books
Farrar, Straus and Giroux
18 West 18th Street, New York 10011

Library of Congress Cataloging-in-Publication Data
Giralt Torrente, Marcos, 1968–
    [Tiempo de vida. English]
    Father and son : a lifetime / Marcos Giralt Torrente ; translated from the
Spanish by Natasha Wimmer. — First American edition.
        pages   cm
    ISBN 978-0-374-27771-0 (cloth : alk. paper) —
    ISBN 978-0-374-71000-2 (e-book)
    1. Giralt Torrente, Marcos, 1968– —Family.   2. Authors, Spanish—
20th century—Family relationships.   3. Fathers and sons—Spain—
Biography.   I. Wimmer, Natasha, translator.   II. Title.

PQ6657.I68 T5413 2014
868'.6403—dc23
                                                            2014013580

Designed by Jonathan D. Lippincott

Farrar, Straus and Giroux books may be purchased for educational, business,
or promotional use. For information on bulk purchases, please contact the
Macmillan Corporate and Premium Sales Department at 1-800-221-7945,
extension 5442, or write to specialmarkets@macmillan.com.

www.fsgbooks.com
www.twitter.com/fsgbooks • www.facebook.com/fsgbooks

10   9   8   7   6   5   4   3   2   1

We have art so that we may not perish by the truth.
—Nietzsche

Father and Son

The same year my father got sick I published a novel in which I killed him.

I've spent whole days, years, studying my father, and resentment has often worked its way into my writing. I've had my revenge. And yet, as Amos Oz writes in his memoir, "he who seeks the heart of the tale in the space between the work and its author is mistaken: the place to look is not the terrain between text and writer, but between text and reader . . ." Much of what I've written was prompted by my father, but I've never written about him. Those were other fathers, other people's fathers.

Now I'm writing about him.

I set down these lines in a notebook in the fall of 2007, when, after months of doubt and of failing repeatedly to come up with any other ideas, I finally accepted that all I could write about was my father. I thought it was a good start, but that was as far as it went; I couldn't continue. The same thing happened with all the other attempts I made in the following days to get past my block.

My plan was to write about the preceding two years, and I simply didn't know how to go about it. I'd done some reading for inspiration, but apparently that only confused me more:

Alone dwells every man and everyone mocks everyone else, and a deserted island is our pain.

(*Book of My Mother*, Albert Cohen)

One day there is life. A man, for example, in the best of health, not even old, with no history of illness. Everything is as it was, as it will always be. He goes from one day to the next, minding his own business, dreaming only of the life that lies before him. And then, suddenly, it happens there is death.

(*The Invention of Solitude*, Paul Auster)

My mother's name was Edna Akin, and she was born in 1910, in the far northwest corner of the state of Arkansas—Benton County—in a place whose actual location I am not sure of and never have been.

(*My Mother, in Memory*, Richard Ford)

I was born in 1896 and my parents were married in 1919.

(*My Father and Myself*, J. R. Ackerley)

My father had lost most of the sight in his right eye by the time he'd reached eighty-six, but otherwise he seemed in phenomenal health for a man his age when he came down with what the Florida doctor diagnosed, incorrectly, as Bell's palsy, a viral infection that causes paralysis, usually temporary, to one side of the face.

(*Patrimony*, Philip Roth)

On the floor in a corner of my study, sticking out from under a pile of other papers, is a shabby old green folder containing a manuscript I believe will tell me a lot about my father and my own past.

(*My Ear at His Heart*, Hanif Kureishi)

These are all first lines from books about real fathers or mothers that I read back then. I also read about mourning (Joan Didion's *The Year of Magical Thinking*); brothers (T. Behrens's *The Monument*); friends (Félix Romeo's *Amarillo*); families (Rick Moody's *The Black Veil*). I even read collections of letters: V. S. Naipaul's *Between Father and Son*.

But I didn't know what book I wanted to write. Or I did know, but I didn't know how to do it. Or I hadn't yet decided what to tell and what not to tell. Or my father's life ultimately wasn't novelistic enough. Or I simply wasn't sure whether it would interest anyone.

I dispensed with the dictatorship of beginnings and wrote isolated chapters, putting off the decision about how to order them.

In Word pages that I filled with uncommon haste, I tried to paint a picture of my father, reaching all the way back to his childhood, his cold, distant father, and the loss of his mother. I tried to put my guilt front and center, setting myself up to seek the redemption that would assuage it; I tried to settle on an illuminating episode that would sum up my experience of him; I tried to weave together random scenes and memories with impressionistic flair; I tried to be cerebral and confront our problem deliberately, leaving no room for poetry.

I wrote: *My father died in February. By December we knew that it was imminent. We thought we were prepared. We had a doctor and a nurse ready to relieve his suffering . . .*

I wrote: *My father was shy, introverted, and melancholy by nature, but that doesn't mean he was sad. He hated any kind of solemnity, including that bred of sadness . . .*

I wrote: *Sometimes those who are about to die rehearse or perform final acts that aren't so much the epitaph that sums up a life as a way of making amends or settling a score that they believe is still pending . . .*

I wrote: *My father was born in August 1940 at 3 Calle San Agustín in Madrid, at the home of his maternal grandparents, where his parents lived temporarily after the war . . .*

I wrote: *I have regrets, yes, but they're of a different nature. It troubles me that much of what he did after he learned that he was ill was a performance that had me in a privileged seat in the audience . . .*

I filled pages, as I've said. But the minute they were filled, I stopped believing in them.

An elegiac portrait of my father wouldn't have been true to my feelings, would have skirted the dark corners from which generous epiphanies might spring . . . ; perhaps I was not so thoroughly in the wrong . . . ; it wasn't easy to come up with an illuminating episode that didn't strain the fidelity that I had pledged to the truth . . . ; a cold, analytic account would have left too much out . . . ; I didn't have the capacity for a great fresco, for anything too detailed that would require me to do research and work out family trees . . . ; nor for the interweaving of intimate scenes, of memory's microscopic flotsam, which anyway was so far from my style.

And then there was everything else:

The why, the justification for writing about us. Everyone has parents, and all parents die. All stories of parents and children are unfinished; all are alike.

The propriety of it, the sense of decorum. Mine and others'.

The challenge, the untested ground. Speaking for the first time in my own voice. An unsettling new feeling: not being able to make things up.

And my father, of course. Would he approve? Did he suspect that I would write about him, as some of the things he said led me to believe, and was he resigned to it? Or beyond suspecting it, did he expect it? I don't know. Those last few months with him were so strange, he shed so many of the habits that he had clung to so atavistically, his boldness was so unexpected, so far from what one could have imagined, that he might have accepted this too. Even wished for it.

All misgivings and insecurities that I should have resolved before sitting down to write.

But there was more. Apart from dropping the mask of fiction, from the difficulty of being my own narrator; apart from my doubts about which moments to choose and how to recount them; apart from my qualms and my fear of betraying him; apart from my limitations, I was missing a leitmotif, for lack of a better word. I harbored the vague intention of making up for all the times when he thought he saw himself in another guise in works of fiction that I'd written; I was guided by the yearning to create an impartial likeness in which, while highlighting his virtues, I didn't hide his flaws, but I lacked the bone and, deeper than that, the marrow. I needed to know where I wanted to go with my story, what I wanted to stress. I lacked the driving idea; it wasn't there, because all I felt was a great void.

Mourning is a strange thing. Mourning is something that you feel only after it passes. Mourning isolates you even from yourself.

I came up with the idea for this book before it was appropriate to take notes for it. For months, as my father faded before my eyes, I knew that I would write about us, and this certainty became my best defense against the flood of feelings in which I was foundering. I felt dazed, and by convincing myself that in the future I would make an accounting of it all, I was able to put off the moment of absorbing what I was experiencing. I took refuge in the present, in my stupor, using it as a barrier. Things were happening, but they weren't fully happening. They were lacking the depths that I refused to contemplate.

When at last my father was gone, I felt like someone who'd been shut up in an air rifle. I was told "Your father lives in you now"; I was told "Go slow, it'll take you a year to recover"; and both pieces of advice seemed equally ridiculous. I decompressed, shooting off into life, and nevertheless, after some time had gone by, both warnings turned out to be true. I've dwelt in nothingness, and all that's left of my father is his memory.

I've become more fragile, sadder, more fearful, skeptical, older. This is the path that's brought me here.

I've thought very little. I haven't asked myself questions. The only unexpected conclusion I've come to is that—pain aside—everything was as it had to be and as we never believed it could be. A circle has closed where there might have been a parting of ways, the widening of a split. Maybe it's the simplicity of this statement that allows me to continue to wear the same deep-sea diver's helmet that I put on when everything began.

How is it possible that something that was about to go one way should have gone another way? Who worked harder to make it happen? Can generous decisions spring from egotistical impulses? Do I have any regrets? Have I put them to rest? Should he have had regrets, as in fact he told me he did? Were they sincere? Were they merited?

The helmet prevents me from answering. Or maybe I'm not fully recovered. Or maybe I am and this is what death is all about: leaving questions unanswered.

So why persist in writing about the two of us?

I've already given some reasons.

Because I tried to go back to writing a novel that I had abandoned when things began to fall apart, and I couldn't do it, and I tried to come up with an idea for another one and I couldn't do that either.

Because writing about something so intimate, so excruciatingly real, seemed a good incentive for recuperating lost routine, the habit of writing.

Because I don't know much more now than I knew when everything started, and establishing the incomplete map of what's known might help me find what eludes me.

Because even though ugly moments will surely slip in, I believe with the conviction of a drowning man that the story is happy; otherwise, I wouldn't tell it.

And maybe it really is true (though this is a trick of mourning) that by making him my own in writing, I cement his memory in me, the only life he has left.

But even all those reasons together aren't enough. Sometimes they're not.

It's hard.

I write more slowly.

Sometimes I attribute it to a loss of discipline, other times to the difficulty of exposing myself like this. I offer up both excuses when friends ask me about my writing, concerned as the months go by. But I'm also convinced that something has broken in me, that something is gone. I'm not talking about the emptiness. I'm not talking about the anguish of loss. I'm talking about the rage with which I used to write.

The memory of him doesn't provoke me, my grievances have vanished, I'm not competing with him, there's no sense in trying to prove anything to him. Nothing affects him anymore, not even what I'm writing now.

How to rid myself of the new feeling of futility that over-comes me when I think about writing?

I read a note in his diary, dated April 14, 2006: "To paint is to make something that didn't exist before, not to erase or to forget but to do and to live, so I plan to keep on with it." Admirable. And yet, as vivid as the act of recognizing his hand-writing in that diary entry is my memory of how dismissive he was one afternoon a few months later, when two of his most loyal friends, thinking that it would entertain him, talked to him about painting.

I can't remember his exact words when they left—how he expressed the distress it caused him to think in the past tense about something to which, until not long ago, he had given the best of himself. Words like: to what end all that effort, to what end all those hours spent struggling over a painting, all those hopes?

I understand it.

We're still bound by the invisible thread of our solitary professions. While I write, I can't imagine him in his studio anymore, but on my computer I listen to music that was his, music that many days he probably listened to as he painted, and I keep working.

I keep working just as he would himself.

In trepidation, taking myself to task, not biting my nails like him, but jiggling my leg nervously, smoking.

I'm trying to understand what we lost, where we got stuck.

There are places I've never been and places I never want to go. I can't tell everything. I have to take a bird's-eye view. I'm try-ing to open a window, show a piece of our life, not its entirety.

My parents were married in 1964. My father was twenty-three and my mother twenty-five. Months earlier, my father had bought an apartment on Calle de la Infanta Mercedes in Madrid with money inherited from his maternal grandfather. The money for the furniture, as was apparently the custom, was contributed by my mother's father. Years later, after he got sick, my father told me that what had attracted him to my mother was her elegant beauty and the imperturbable mystery of her gaze. From the time he was twenty, he had been travel-ing around Europe; he had lived in Amsterdam, London, and Paris, and nowhere had he lacked for female companionship, as photographs of the era attest. My mother, meanwhile, still lived at home and hadn't had a boyfriend, properly speaking, but rather romantic friendships with a sailor, a German, a poet friend of her brother's. I don't know what attracted her to my father: his blond hair, the fact that he was a painter . . . Any-way, they got married, and then they left for Brazil, where they lived for two years in São Paulo. My mother didn't work. My father had shown his paintings at galleries in Madrid and London and Amsterdam, and he participated in the São Paulo Biennial. There are pictures of the two of them, dressed up, at dinners and parties, restaurants, galleries, the Spanish em-bassy; there are pictures of them with friends in private homes or on the beach; there are pictures of them as tourists in Bra-sília or Bahia or São Paulo, in sandals and jeans; there are pictures of them in the jungle, where they lived with the Karajá Indians. In all the pictures they are smiling, and in some they're even mugging for the camera. It's the dawn of their marriage.

In Brazil my father met the woman who—once he was separated from my mother—would be his wife for the last twenty years of his life. But that's another story, and it came later.

The dawn of their marriage was prolonged after their return to Madrid in 1966. My father paints and shows his work. They have no responsibilities yet; they don't have me. They're always coming and going. Friends visit: painter friends, writer friends. Friends—some of them—whose outlandish appearance in the Madrid of the day could stop traffic. In the photographs I have they look more relaxed than in the earlier ones, their displays of happiness toned down. And yet it seems an artificial calm, as if they're playing at being grown-ups. My father in an armchair, with a glass of whiskey in his hand, and my mother behind him, leaning against the back of the chair with an arm around his shoulders. They go through some hard times, times of uncertainty, when money is scarce. At some point between 1966 and 1968, when I'm born, my father goes to work as a page designer at the newspaper *Informaciones*. At some point between 1966 and 1968, when I'm born, my mother finds work as a buyer for a textile chain. Years later, my father confesses to me that he couldn't understand my mother's incredible nonchalance, her lack of concern about practical matters; they might have no money to eat the next day and it wouldn't bother her. Years later, my mother tells me that my father didn't last long at the paper, he couldn't stand it. My father steals things from stores, including food, steaks that he slips under his arm. He wins a prize for prints at the Tokyo Biennale, spends a season in Paris on a scholarship from the Juan March Foundation. But they're happy, or so it seems to me, and soon I arrive to confirm it. It has taken them four years, and not because they've done anything to prevent it.

Days before I'm born, my father paints the room that will be mine and finishes the portrait of my mother that hangs in it. After the birth, a hemorrhage leaves my mother on the verge of death, and days later, some poorly administered antibiotics leave me on the verge of death. I'm given an emergency baptism in the bathroom, without my father's knowledge and with my mother's consent.

During a not-so-short period of my early life, I suppose that my father was a more daily presence than I was able to observe in other stages that served me as the model for our common past. If only because he worked at home, his presence had to be more constant than my mother's, since she always went out to work.

I remember a day in the place where we lived until I was three, when he brought me to the room where he painted and had me color some circles on a painting; I remember that in the mornings, on the way to the school bus, he recounted the adventures of a monkey called Manolo, who went to school like me; I remember that I loved the story so much that if my mother or the nanny was with me, I asked them to tell it, and either they couldn't do it very well or they hardly ever had to substitute for my father, because the name Manolo always reminds me of him. I remember that one afternoon—and it must be a fairly early memory because I have the sense that I experienced this all from a playpen—he went out for a minute to buy something and I burst into tears when, despite all his soothing words, his absence was more terrifying than anticipated; I remember how impatiently he tried to calm me and the attempts he made—like those he would later make in response to any complaint of mine—to downplay my unhappiness, suggest that I was exaggerating and blowing things out of proportion. I remember the afternoons at our second apartment that he spent teaching me how to ride a bike, how he would pick me up from school with our first dog, and for a few seconds, before going out through the glass doors, I could watch him without being seen; I remember looking for slugs in the yard together; and—it sounds made up, but it isn't—how one day he showed me the newspaper and told me that Picasso had died. I remember one night at our next place with some of his friends—they must have been high—when we divided up into teams and made a game of throwing felt dolls onto a Velcro-covered trapeze; I remember the first time I ran away from school and how, when I got home, he punished me for the first and only time; I remember writing, at his request, the names of my friends on a painting he was making; I remember many afternoons in his studio, the two of us painting, he with an eye on my scribbles, which he gathered up meticulously and kept in folders.

Now that I think about it, though, that early stage wasn't so linear, nor was his presence so constant. I know, for example, that in the six years and three apartments spanned by the memories I've just recounted, he lived for a long time in Paris and then in Essaouira, Morocco, where my mother and I visited him twice. The problems in the marriage had already appeared, and though it's likely that both my parents thought it could be saved, my father's dissatisfaction, his instinct to liberate himself from the burden that my mother and I represented in a milieu—that of his painter friends—where family responsibilities were the exception, took inexorable hold of him in the end. Nevertheless, the fact that I have these memories, and no recollection of discontent or unhappiness, leads me to think that it wasn't yet the problem it later became for me. Either my mother managed to cover up his absences by giving them a convincing patina of normality, or I unconsciously compensated for them by granting him an unassailable place in my life.

In fact, not even for the next four years (1975, 1976, 1977, 1978) does the landscape change much. My father is gone more and more often, disappearing completely from my daily life for long stretches, but he keeps his studio, and though later I learn that his relationship with my mother was almost nonexistent, there are no serious repercussions for me. My mother keeps things normal even when they're not; my mother ensures that my father is still my father, leaving no room for doubts, complaints, or dangerous fissures.

Where do they lead, these few memories I'm able to dredge up? Where are they taking me? They lead to an afternoon when I hear loud voices in my mother's bedroom, and when I open the door, frightened, I see my mother on her knees, in tears, and my father brandishing the empty frame of a painting he's just smashed on the floor, the very one on which he'd asked me to write the names of my friends. I remember that I closed the door and that, after a period of time I can't specify, when we passed each other in the hall and I asked him where he was going, he said to the movies and left, slamming the door. Though my mother still insists that he came back to say goodbye, the only thing I remember is a postcard, of two Angora cats, that I received a few weeks later from Paris; and later another one of an old cycling poster; and a few more that arrived every so often until, a few months later, he came back and took away his easel, boxes of paints, pencils, aerosols, stretchers, rolls of canvas, drawing paper, notebooks, scraps for making collages; and what had been his studio became my huge bedroom, the bedroom of a privileged only child. My father was gone from our daily life, and not even then did it come as a shock. My mother was there to soften the blow, and he came back occasionally, sometimes even sleeping in the room that had been mine before I took possession of his studio.

My father comes and buys me clogs like his; my father comes and—reluctantly—buys me a doll that I've requested; my father comes and buys me an Elvis Presley album. We spend the summers together too. Strange summers on Formentera.

My mother and I in one house with assorted guests, and my father and his guests in another house, sometimes next door.

And that's not all. I get used to other men coming to the house. Actually, it's just one man. I still don't know whether he was my mother's boyfriend, though I suppose that's the word that best describes him. He brings me things, pets; I'm fond of him, and we make a life with him. More than with my father.

And that's not all. Since 1970, my mother and father have worked together. My mother is the codirector of an art gallery in Madrid and my father is one of her painters. These are fertile years for both of them. They're at the heart of Madrid's cultural scene. My mother wears a miniskirt, is admired and desired by almost everyone, and my father is a prominent member of a generation of young painters. At a show of his in 1974, everything sells. And the buyers are other painters.

And that's not all. Tired, she claims, of the clashes between the other director and the owner, my mother leaves the gallery in 1975, and three years later my father leaves too, after a falling-out with the remaining director for having favored a rival painter. My mother goes to work for a collector, but the job doesn't last long and it takes her a while to find something else. Meanwhile, my father is heading for a crisis. Without the gallery where he's shown for the last eight years, he lacks the confidence to face up to his career. Financial problems overwhelm him, and his visits aren't as relaxed or as frequent as before. I remember one afternoon when he comes with us to sell a gold coin that someone has given me. He's tense. I imagine that he'd like to be able to help and is ashamed that he can't. This fixation and his air of bitterness will become familiar over the course of our lives.

This is 1978.

But my mother recovers. She reinvents herself. She works

briefly in television and then more steadily in radio, and immediately we sense my father's relief. His bitterness lifts and
he begins to visit us regularly again. He's still painting and
showing his work, though not with the old fanfare. His former gallery is the most important in Madrid and he's lost the
chance to show there. Intrigues are mounted against him, too,
by young critics who champion his rival. He doubts himself,
watches others triumph, and gets discouraged. Sometimes he's
strong and keeps working, and sometimes he gets distracted
and loses himself in female labyrinths. I come across scraps of
this: a picture of him naked with two women; an afternoon
when he's admitted to the hospital with kidney trouble, and
when my mother and I arrive, we're told at the reception desk
that his wife has just left; the apologies of the guard at the
apartment complex where a married female friend lives for
having mistaken him for a thief when he climbed out the
window the night before . . . None of it hurts; I simply remember it. Just as it doesn't hurt that it's my mother I see
when I get up, my mother who helps me with my homework
and goes to school to talk to my teachers. At the same time—
probably due at least in part to my mother's prodding—he's
always there at critical moments. I come down with rheumatic
fever and he increases his visits. The nights of my mother's
radio show he usually stays with me into the early-morning
hours. I'm with him the day I have an attack of peritonitis,
and he pays the surgeon with one of his paintings. It doesn't
even have to be anything serious. In the summer he comes to
swim at our community pool, sometimes he stays for dinner
when my mother's father is there, and many Sundays he brings
his father for lunch. If I want something, he does his best to
get it for me. Then he jokingly makes a big deal about it and
says that all I have to do is ask him for the smallest thing and
there he is on bended knee, but the truth is that he does come

through (*the smallest thing, on bended knee*, the times I must have heard him say that . . .).

This is 1978, the year of the constitutional referendum. Behind us are the assassination of Carrero Blanco, Franco's death, and the elections of '77. The effects of these events are still being felt in our house. The Christmas of the Carrero Blanco assasination, my cousins and I are playing guessing games, and when it's my turn, I mime an explosion; the night of November 21, 1975, while my father is in Paris, the phone rings off the hook, and later friends come over. The next day, my mother gets me dressed and sends me to school, but before I can get out the front door of the building, the door-man stops me, long-faced. Around this time, we attend two Communist Party of Spain gatherings, one clandestine and the second by then legal, and we watch the king's proclamation on television. Stories fly about the guerrillas of Fuerza Nueva and Bandera Roja. I have an album of Civil War songs, and I learn "The Internationale." In '77 I'm taught in school to make a basic gelatin print and I print flyers asking people to vote for José Bergamín, who is running for senator on the Republican Left ticket. All of this I essentially live through with my mother, but my mother is a monarchist, my father a republican, and I— like my father—am a republican. I decide this at a traffic light in Plaza de Castilla one afternoon when the two of us are out in his blue Dyane 6. My father has a pack of cigarettes on the dashboard (Lola, they're called), and what he says is more venal than rational, but I get it. I want to get it, to share this with him.

Then there's God. My mother has taught me to pray, and that same afternoon, with the pack of Lola on the dashboard, I listen to my father argue against the existence of God and life after death. Here, however, I stand my ground. Where are the grandmothers I never met? I agree with him, I try to convince myself that after death there is nothing, but I'm not being entirely honest. In fact, though I hide it from him, for years I still keep trying to believe. When we visit a cathedral or a church, I cross myself, and he can't help smiling. He's moved by it. I'm sure it irritates him that we aren't alike in this regard, that he hasn't convinced me, but he's moved by it.

Before going on, I should pause here. When coolly catalogued, the facts of the past lose their distinctiveness and come to seem interchangeable. A catalogue like the one I've been making does a better job than any digression would of reflecting the transitory nature of life, the nothing that everything becomes when death makes its appearance; still, emphasizing the latter point—important as it is—is not my only goal.

A life, though fragile and ephemeral, is so singular that it comes as a surprise that it should be the result of an act of intercourse. The contrast between the trivial randomness with which two bodies unite and the meaning that the life to which that union may give rise assumes for the person who possesses it obsessed me for a while. On alcohol-fueled nights, surrounded by friends, the calculation of the approximate dates of our origination filled me with hilarity and vertigo. More than our births, it amused and dismayed me to conjure up the moment nine months earlier when we were conceived. Why did our parents' bodies come together on that particular day at that particular time? Maybe it was dinner out and a few drinks; maybe they had been on a trip to the country and it was the coda to a summer outing; maybe they had fought and this was how they made up. But what would have happened if they hadn't taken a trip, hadn't gone out to dinner, hadn't fought, hadn't slept together that night? More than any other paradox, the tremendous futility of these questions encapsulated for me the tragedy of the human condition, the arbitrariness of our fate.

When does life begin to be subjected to a multitude of factors capable of altering it, of channeling it in a certain direction?

I'm the result of an act of intercourse that took place at the end of May 1967. I don't know the circumstances, and I don't care to know them. Nor do I know what caused the bodies of my father's parents to unite in November 1939, though here I can take some license: they had spent the war apart, she in Biarritz and he in Madrid, and after their reunion, I imagine that whatever their inclinations, their carnal relations must have been frequent.

I'll have to go back in time if I want to sketch a comprehensible portrait of my father.

His birthplace itself is revealing: in Madrid, across from the Cortes, in a grand block of apartments built at the turn of the twentieth century to be inhabited by families of the Madrid haute bourgeoisie, among which his was certainly not the least prominent. I'm told that I visited the place, but the truth is that I have no memory of it. Or no memory of the inside, since the building still stands. From the photographs I've seen, I know that it possessed all the attributes of the opulent homes of the day. Spacious rooms, gold-framed mirrors, rugs from the Royal Tapestry Factory . . . In theory it belonged to his maternal grandparents, but just as his parents took refuge there after the war, other family members came to spend some time or settled there more or less permanently. It must have been a happy place, because his mother's family was happy. Happy and not at all conventional, despite their standing.

I know, for example, that my great-grandfather had a brother who was a morphine addict and another who never left the house or even his bed, where he spent his days reading travel books surrounded by maps, and that my great-grandfather looked after both of them, administering their fortunes. On my great-grandmother's side, an emblematic case is that of a rather quiet and retiring brother—so quiet that strangers imagined he was mute—who, after a life as a model bachelor, appeared at his mother's house one day with a former maid and three boys already in long pants, whom he introduced as his children. When my great-great-grandmother, beyond scandalized, asked why he'd had relations with the maid, his answer was "Because she brought up my meals every day . . ."

Socially, both branches of the maternal side of my father's family constituted two unique but related versions of the haute bourgeoisie of the Madrid of the era. They weren't industrialists or government officials or professionals. My great-grandfather's family came from the north of Castilla and boasted noble origins, though my great-grandfather's fortune, when my father was born, was founded on speculation in securities and real estate; my great-grandmother's family on the maternal side was from Madrid and on the paternal side from a mountain village that my great-great-grandfather had left at the end of the nineteenth century to come and open a perfumery, which in its day was the best in the capital, one of those businesses petulantly displaying a sign reading OFFICIAL PURVEYORS OF THE ROYAL FAMILY. The differences between my great-grandfather's family of landowners and my great-grandmother's family of tradespeople were amplified by various shades of behavior that aren't worth elaborating upon here. What matters is that both represented a way of life that was soon to disappear, a way of life for which neither family—whether out of ineptitude or because of copious wartime losses—was able to find a substitute. The truth is that my father never knew this life in all its glory, but rather at the beginning of its decline. And yet, that world—unequivocally bourgeois, but with sufficient outlets for the cultivation of taste and judgment—was the lost paradise to which he always dreamed of returning. A paradise that was equal parts bourgeois stability and the happiness mentioned above.

I stress happiness to underscore one of my father's defining characteristics: his yearning to be happy, to recover the lightness that the passage of time tends to make more difficult, less permanent, as well as to distinguish the atmosphere of faded but cheerful prosperity that reigned in the home of his mother's parents from that of the home into which he moved with his parents shortly after his birth. If my great-grandparents' house reflected the taste of the haute bourgeoisie of the 1890s, my grandparents' exemplified the preferences of the bourgeoisie that established itself in the postwar period. A new brick building with square windows ranged symmetrically on each facade, it was chosen with the needs of my grandmother—who had heart trouble—in mind. The apartment had to be on the second floor, and the building had to have an elevator. Before the war they'd had another apartment, but perhaps because its contents were lost when Madrid was under siege, almost all the furniture was bought new. What wasn't new was my grandparents' marriage. They already had two daughters and very little in common. My grandfather was born in Barcelona, and when he turned twenty, he settled in Madrid with one of his brothers to run a glass factory belonging to his father, which he would later leave to start a ceramics factory. He was a solitary man, obsessed with upholding the legacy of his ancestors, as well as the youngest (and probably the least business-minded) son of a family of Catalan industrialists, and the shock for my grandmother—in whose family almost no one had ever worked—must have been brutal. She never understood that for her husband, there was no life beyond the walls of his factory, nor did she grow accustomed to his stern ways. As a result, she threw herself into caring for her children, and most of all my father, the youngest and the only boy. So devoted was she to him that she had a window cut in the wall that separated their bedrooms in order to watch over him at night during the long spells of illness that kept her bedridden.

The closeness of their relationship was the key to my father's insecurity, especially from the moment he found himself prematurely deprived of her. He was twelve when his mother died, and his father proved unable to change his ways to give him the support he needed. With the years, the distance between them only grew, and just as emphatically as my grandfather expected him to follow in his footsteps, my father began to make it clear that he wouldn't. He finished high school with mediocre grades, and he didn't go to college to study engineering—which is what his father would have liked—or even art, a compromise that wasn't considered, despite the fact that since he was fourteen, it had been clear that painting was his calling. My father was not the son my grandfather had hoped for, and busy as he was establishing his ceramics factory, he had neither the time nor the sensitivity to engage with him. Someone more open, less single-minded, might have found other ways to involve him, but my grandfather couldn't even rise to the occasion when at one point my father offered to help design some dishes. When my father told me about this, rushing through the story in his eagerness to be done with it, and probably still bitter, he couldn't help adding that the proposal he had vainly presented, inspired by Scandinavian design, would have had a better chance of succeeding than the generic pieces my grandfather produced.

The break came when my father, still a minor, requested his legal emancipation in order to travel to London to study painting. My grandfather granted it, and for good measure, possibly with the intention of getting him to change his mind, disinherited him. This didn't affect my father much, since shortly afterward my grandfather went bankrupt so spectacularly that he had to flee abroad, pursued by his creditors. What my father couldn't forgive was that in an earlier desperate attempt to avoid ruin, he had spent the money that my father and his sisters had inherited from their mother, of which he was trustee.

But I've written about this already—though in a different form—in my second novel.

I don't know exactly what my father thought of his own father; he was never explicit about it. I know that once, when someone took it for granted that he didn't love him, he denied it vehemently, but the fact is that he reproached him for many things: for his coldness, for his sadness, for not supporting him in his artistic career, for not making an effort to understand him, for rejecting his advice, for valuing his businesses above all else and then losing them.

And then there was the absence of his mother, like a perpetual question mark, nagging at his memory with different versions of what might have been.

I've never been in therapy, and my knowledge of psychology goes no further than what I learned in a college class, but I suppose that together these stories present a fairly convincing explanation of the two traits that, beyond painting, defined my father's life: a tendency to lose himself in the labyrinth of the female minotaur, where his need to seek the shelter of strong women lay hidden; and a terrible fear of the future, of having the rug suddenly pulled out from under him. Add to that a perhaps excessive sensitivity, and two plus one is three.

As Joan Didion says in *The Year of Magical Thinking*, we never stop telling ourselves stories. It's our way of being in the world, of capturing life. I don't know when I started to plot the story that I've just told, made up of bits taken from here and there. Probably when I began to sense that the clay from which my father was molded was not so solid.

But we were in 1978, and I've said that I would stay aloft.

Nineteen seventy-eight is the year of my First Communion. No one pushes me, though the fact is that it's no simple process. As I was baptized under emergency circumstances, the procedure first has to be repeated in front of an ecclesiastical notary. My father attends the ceremony—at which I renounce Satan and all his pomp and works—but not the Communion itself. I don't care: it's not in Madrid; he has an excuse. I'm not very sure myself about what I've done. My conversion is relative. I want to believe the way my mother believes, and sometimes I pray and cross myself, but I never go back to take Communion again and certainly not to confess.

The following years bring few changes, but important ones. In 1979 and 1980 my father still makes the occasional halfhearted attempt at family life with us. He even travels with us. To Extremadura with one set of friends, to the Mar Menor with another. I don't know whether he does this of his own accord or whether the appearances he makes are the tribute my mother claims for me. Whatever the case, he shows up, and though sometimes I may notice that his mind is elsewhere, his lack of enthusiasm is never something he turns against me: it has to do with his relationship with my mother. And yet I'm part of the same package, and it's inevitable that he should associate me with her. The world that she's woven so that their separation goes unnoticed begins to come apart, and despite their efforts, there are many moments when I miss him, when I sense that he's hiding another life, other appetites, and I guess at the lie. Once, he tells me that he's in Andalucía and a friend of my mother's happens to tell me that she ran into him in London on the same day. I notice that he doesn't contribute to my keep, that he doesn't give me money, that it's hard to involve him in plans he doesn't devise himself, that he's evasive.

School. I'm not doing well at the public school where he chose to have me enrolled five years earlier (I'm an oddball), and my mother moves me to a private school with a well-deserved reputation for being liberal. She alone makes the decisions that concern me. My father has gradually bowed out; either he doesn't feel he has the authority to impose his views, or he trusts my mother's judgment. From now on, that's the way it will be; though he may criticize her at times, though he's driven to distraction—as I will be, years later—by what he would call her exaggerated enthusiasms, her patrician sense of life, he'll always let her be the one to choose how things are done or undone. He's infuriated by her disregard for material things, her essential optimism, her tendency to be a dreamer, her failure to consider that everything could take a turn for the worse, but since he has no stability to offer us, he cuts himself off. He wants us to save what he can't give us, he wants us to be prudent, he doesn't want to have to worry about us, he wants us to be safe so that he will be too.

My mother and I do spend money. Without a second thought. We eat out whenever we want, we have a maid, and we take taxis everywhere, but the truth is that we lack for nothing. She makes enough. She works and makes money. She has grown up too. She may not save, she may not plan for tomorrow, but she has liberated herself from the world she shared with my father and created her own world, with new friends. Everything is going well. What does my father have to complain about? He thinks he knows her, and he's terrified by her levity, the way she seems to make decisions without considering the consequences. Whenever he can, he seeks my complicity to criticize her. It bothers him that by nature I'm as relaxed as she is, and he tries to reform me.

My mother's world of dreams. My father's paralyzing hyperrealism. I'm torn—my head and my frustrated desires with my father, my heart and my day-to-day life with my mother. Sometimes I ally myself with my father, but it's my mother I live with, and I simply don't understand my father's dissatisfaction, his dutiful lack of enthusiasm when he comes to see us.

In early 1980 my father shows at a fleetingly successful gallery, and a few months later he leaves on a Fulbright to spend a year in New York. The day of his departure he gives me conflicting reasons for why I shouldn't come to the airport, and I suspect that either he isn't traveling alone or he's being seen off by someone he doesn't want me to meet. I get a postcard of fake UFOs flying over the Twin Towers, I get a postcard of a miniature explorer shrunken by natives, I get a postcard of an Art Deco teapot, I get a postcard of graffiti. Those are the ones I kept; I don't think there were any others. No letter. Occasionally he calls me. Hurried conversations in which he barrages me with questions.

Since he left, it's been agreed that I'll visit him, but although it's my mother's understanding that she's coming too, he thinks I'll be coming alone. I don't know whether it's a misunderstanding or whether one of them wasn't honest with the other in previous conversations. The fact is that when my mother and I arrive to spend Christmas, it's clear from the start that my father doesn't want her there. They don't tell me this, but I sense it. I sleep with my father in the double bed, and my mother sleeps on a mattress on the floor. I remember one afternoon when they leave me in the loft to have a private conversation. Even so, my father takes us on long excursions, showing us the city as if nothing is wrong. He buys me John Lennon's *Double Fantasy*, he buys me an electronic flipper game, he buys me some eye-catching yellow radio headphones, he buys me snow boots. At Bloomingdale's, the night before we go back, my mother gets me a brown corduroy polo jacket, and she exits with a black digital watch that—tired of waiting to be helped—my father takes without paying. They try to act normal in front of me; at moments they probably even forget that it's an act. But that trip is key to the severing of the final emotional ties between them, because years later they continue to bring it up, he still angry and she still hurt.

The years 1981, 1982, and 1983 are confused in my memory. Either too many things happen or I begin to be too conscious of what's happening. I've grown up; I'm more aware. I'm not a mere witness anymore. In '81 I spend the night of the coup with my mother and some neighbors, while my father is still in New York. When he returns months later, he doesn't let me know in advance. I sense motives related to those of his departure the year before, but this time when I see him, I'm filled with silent anger. He pretends to have arrived the previous night, but he contradicts himself. It bothers me, but I don't say anything. He brings me the life jacket from the plane and albums by the Talking Heads, the B-52s, Split Enz, and Yellowman, but I hardly thank him. His lie bothers me, and it bothers me that I've been displaced. It's the beginning of the silences between us. The silences happen when he hides something from me that I know he's hiding, he knows that I know it, and I know that he knows that I know it. If he betrays me, I immediately sense his betrayal and he immediately senses that I've sensed his betrayal. It isn't even necessary for him to make a mistake or for me to hide my disappointment. All we have to do is exchange glances.

It's the beginning of the silences between us.

But we also take our first trip alone together. A trip to London, paid for by my mother. This trip and another the following year to Paris and Amsterdam, also my mother's treat, will be the only trips we take until twenty years later. I learn to travel with him, to visit museums with him. I learn to despise all chauvinism with him, not to entrench myself in the familiar, to appreciate variety. I learn how important painting is to him, the pleasure that he gets from looking at art.

And life goes on, and he continues to visit us when he feels like it, and once again he stays with me some nights when my mother has her radio show. Our apartment isn't the same one that he left—or maybe was kicked out of. We've moved to another considerably smaller one, but the furniture and almost all the paintings are the same, since he hardly took anything with him when he left. Regarding the justice of this fact, as well as the payment my mother gave him when she sold the first apartment, they will never see eye to eye.

One night when he's with me he brings a female friend along. He's never done it before, and I'm conscious of the fact that my mother wouldn't like it. What surprises me most is that he points out anything of value with proprietary pride, including my only asset: a drawing my mother asked Miró to make for me when, in '72, there was an exhibition of his work at the gallery she ran.

The friend is the friend he met in Brazil.

My father did almost no work in New York, and though he tries, he does hardly any when he returns to Madrid. It's the dawning of a crisis from which—because it sidelines him during crucial years when the art market is taking off—he won't easily recover. He seeks alternatives, works in the studio of a designer, and goes to Galicia for a few months to fix up and decorate a colonial-era house. From Galicia he writes me letters in which he calls me *turkey-cock*, *lovey*, or *bratty-cakes*, remembers to send his love to my mother, and reminds me to be good. One of them ends like this: "I don't expect you to write, but maybe someday you'll have something you want to tell your dad, or ask him (you can always trust your father, who would love to be your best friend.)"

Clearly, he's at a low point. This is only confirmed the two times I go to see him. Once, when I've been there for a few days, a female friend of his arrives and a problem arises that at the time I'm unable to fully appreciate. Since work is being done on the house, there are only two bedrooms. My father and I sleep in one of them, and the owner's grown-up children sleep in the other. My father tries to get me to move in with them, but I refuse: even with someone else in the room, it seems more natural to me to sleep with them than with two strangers. My father gets angry, grumbles, but accepts it in the end. Two clashing forms of logic: a child's and an adult's.

The next year, 1982, is hectic. Hectic because lots of things—contradictory things—happen. Hectic because their effect on me is mixed. Hectic because 1982 stretches on, turning into 1983. In '82 we visit Paris and Amsterdam; in '82 I go out at night, march in protests, and wear a little black circle-A anarchist pin; in '82 I spend the summer in England and buy myself a pair of plaid pants, boots, and a leather jacket; in '82 I make short-lived plans with some friends to form a band. I tell my father about it one Sunday when we're at lunch with my mother in a Chinese restaurant, and though at first he can't help making a joke of it, he ends up becoming our biggest champion, as is always the case when behind some plan of mine he senses an itch to escape my mother's influence. In '82 my father adopts the habit of picking me up at school some days and returning me the next morning after the two of us spend the night at the studio where he lives and works. In the evening, after dinner at a restaurant, he takes me to shows or to the movies or—during the season—to a bullfight. I remember seeing Picasso and Mondrian and El Greco and Dalí, and especially a Kurt Schwitters show that for a few evenings inspires me to forget the black Olivetti typewriter on which I've begun to write and throw myself into making collages à la Kurt Schwitters: I remember *Quest for Fire*; I remember *City of Women*; I remember *Fitzcarraldo*; I remember a Monty Python movie and a revival of *Eraserhead*. All in all, in '82 we see quite a bit of each other; I bask in the novel male camaraderie and imprint on my brain attitudes that I will make my own, but it's also an era in which the silences between us grow thicker. One day, on what pretext I can't remember, he brings me to an apartment to which he has a key, and on the doorstep, just before we go in, he warns me that I'll see paintings and pieces of furniture that belong to him, which he's loaned to the owner for a story in a design magazine. Weeks later, after he picks me up from school, instead of sleeping at his studio, we sleep at that same apartment, this time with the owner present. It's the friend he met in Brazil, whom just over a year ago he'd brought to my mother's apartment.

I spend two or three nights there, sleeping in one bedroom or another, depending on shifting criteria, until for reasons I can't explain, the evenings with him become less and less frequent. He no longer invites me to spend the night. He no longer comes to pick me up from school.

And yet he doesn't break ties completely. There are silences, mutual misunderstandings, but in hindsight they look more like a foretaste of what's to come than a permanent reality. He comes over when he chooses, spends the evening, and leaves in a hurry, briskly, as if escaping from invisible snares.

But there's more.

A parenthesis.

At some point between '82 and '83, my mother, who has a crowded calendar and goes out a lot at night, becomes involved in a romantic relationship with one of her suitors, a writer by trade. At some point between '82 and '83, my father asks my mother to be his guarantor in the purchase of a ground-floor apartment for sale in the two-story building where the friend he met in Brazil has her apartment. My mother is prepared to give him the money, but suddenly it's the friend he met in Brazil who doesn't want him to have the place. My father is incensed. One Saturday he asks me to come with him to her house, and we take his things. The break deepens the depression from which he's been suffering for years. He paints very little, his income is minimal, it distresses him to have missed the boat on the new times that are shaking up the art world, he's probably drinking too much. At some point between '82 and '83, my mother gets worried, and during a conversation one night, after decreeing that his studio isn't the best place to lead an orderly life, she invites him to come live with us. My mother is still with the writer, but he lives in France, not Madrid, and so for a while my father is once again a daily presence in my life. In the morning he gets up at the same time as I do, shares the bathroom with me, teaches me to shave. I get used to his smell, a sharp smell that I now recognize on myself. One afternoon, during an argument I have with my mother, he takes her side and hits me. At night we sleep in the same room, in separate beds.

By now it's '83. It's summer. I spend July in Ibiza, the guest of a friend's father, and August in the Basque Country with my mother and her writer boyfriend. My father is left alone in Madrid. Our stay in the Basque Country, conceived as a kind of test marriage, is a failure. I return to Madrid a few days before the end of August, and my mother arrives three days later, after ending her relationship with the writer. Over the past months I've fantasized about the possibility that my parents will get back together, and this might be the ideal moment if it weren't for the fact that in our absence my father has reconciled with the friend he met in Brazil.

Still, it's a while before matters take their course. He's very grateful to my mother, and I suppose that a sudden exit strikes him as being in poor taste. Until October or November, the days blur. I can't remember how quickly or slowly the parenthesis is closed. My father appears and disappears, and I'm out almost every weekend with my first girlfriend, the daughter of a friend of my mother's. We sleep together one night when for whatever reason it's my father who's home. He lets me in after midnight as I fumble with my key, and though I don't say a thing, he jokes that he hopes I haven't made him a grandfather.

This will be the last time he spends the night. Everything changes as his visits grow further apart, and he becomes more and more reluctant to participate in family plans not dictated by him. He's worked things out with the friend he met in Brazil. He has a foot in two worlds, and he gives most where most is demanded of him. His variability increases, as do the silences and the mutual lack of enthusiasm. The times he chooses to see me are dead moments, interruptions of daily routine. My discontent grows gradually, but busy as I am, I don't have much time for him either. I come and go, see shows on my own, throw myself fully into my romance.

An unexpected event arrives to change everything, making what was once an occasional rumble of annoyance more cutting. Suddenly we're broke. My mother's radio contract expires and the program sponsors don't renew it. She's out of work. We have no savings, and our financial situation is worrisome. We give up the maid and get some help from my mother's father, but it isn't enough. My mother informs her friends of her situation, and every Sunday she goes through the help wanted sections with me and we send out CVs, but nothing happens. My father is aware of what's going on, of course. I make sure of that, but the only result is that he makes himself scarce. There's an element in his attitude of getting his own back, of *I told you so*, of shamefaced compunction at having no other solution than flight. I don't know what kind of help I expected from him, but this is definitely not it. For the months that my mother's troubles last, he vanishes, doesn't even call. My rage grows. For the first time, I feel full force what it's like to be left in the lurch. The few times that we speak, I can't be natural. I judge his life from afar. He doesn't have money, he claims; he can't help us, he insists. Whereas all I can see is that he's removed himself from the mess, and I doubt the truth of his excuses. It's the real estate boom of the mid-eighties and with the friend he met in Brazil he buys apartments to fix up and sell. The initial capital is hers, but the work, the search for properties, the renovation decisions, and the oversight are all his. And he never sees the fruits of his labor. He's a worker without pay. He works for her in exchange for imagining that he has something to fall back on. His excuses aren't good enough for me, considering that my mother and I have nothing, but more than anything it's his desertion that hurts. Even though I sense that he isn't untouched by it, that it's at once the result and cause of deep suffering, I feel let down.

This is how things will be from now on.

Could he really have helped us in 1984? Today, March 22, 2009, as I revise what I wrote many months ago, I have my doubts. Was he really absent as often as I remember? Should I have concerned myself so much with our financial problems? Was it my place to take him to task?

This is a story of two people, though I'm the only one telling it. My father wouldn't tell it. My father kept almost everything to himself.

Sometimes the responsibility frightens me. I try to strip away all embellishment, set down the memories exactly as they come into my head, but obviously I can't avoid making some decisions.

Up until now I'd never written in my own voice. I had written *fictionally* about reality, as one always does, but it wasn't *my* reality and I wasn't the one narrating. It's a new and confusing feeling. With fiction, you can say anything. In your own voice, either you're tempted to leave things out or you miss being able to make things up. I've passed through both states in previous pages.

Really, though, one of my fears is not having anything to add to what I've written in other books—books that were fiction, about other people who weren't me, but into which I poured myself.

I don't include my first book. In my first book, a collection of short stories, I wasn't even conscious that I was writing about reality. I had read, or been warned by someone—an older writer, maybe my own grandfather—that it isn't a good idea to make one's first novel a self-portrait, that it blocks the imagination and creates vices that are hard to shake, and so convinced was I of this that in the book's stories I shunned personal experience and borrowed only some unimportant traits of mine—poor eyesight, for example, or certain habits—to distinguish the different narrators. To none of them did I give anything that was truly mine.

It wasn't until my first novel that I equipped myself with a spelunker's helmet to climb down into known depths. And even when I did, it wasn't intentional. I wanted to write about the insecurities of childhood, and as usual, my desire to write preceded the invention of a story. I remember being paralyzed, unable to come up with anything, until before I realized it, the childhood I was trying to elaborate began to take on elements of my own. The narrator, an adult narrator looking back on his childhood, was an only child, and the epicenter of his family was his mother, with whom he lived and shared the ambivalent memory of an absent father. I lent him the feelings of dread and the thoughts I had at the time, but that was all I took from my own experiences. Or at least so I thought while I was writing it.

My father, however, saw things differently.

Just recently I found out that he was very upset by it, and though the person who told me this isn't especially trustworthy, in this case the information is credible because I'd previously gotten the same impression. This was very early on, the same day he'd told me he was reading the book. One more drop in the sea of information that flowed between us without need of words.

When you're an only child, when you don't have the mirror of siblings, any insecurity about who you are must seem greater than it would if you'd had them, if you'd grown up alongside someone who was shaped by the same influences, who had the same parents and yet was still sharply different from them and—of course—from you. When there are no siblings to turn to, parents are all we have, our only reference, our only vantage point. Everything begins and ends in us, and phenomena like betrayal, love, admiration, or duty are felt with greater intensity. Bonds are stronger or leave more of a mark, and very often it's hard to distinguish between what's particular to us and what's inherited. We have no one to compare ourselves to; loneliness chokes us. Who do we share things with or unburden ourselves to? Who do we go to with questions, answers, accusations? How do we get a measure of distance? How do we construct a balanced account from memory when all we have is a single gaze, and that gaze is shaded—slanted, too—by our own unique selves? When you don't have siblings everything seems designed especially for you. The danger is that we tend to magnify things, and that from each word spoken to us, each look or slight, each occurrence witnessed (or sensed or reported or even just imagined) we draw infinite conclusions. The result is that we're bound even tighter and we're wrong more often too. It may be that we place too much importance on our parents, that the necessary break is harder for us, and it may be that sometimes we don't value them as much as they deserve. Everything is likely to cause us more pain, and most of all our own singular selves. We're alone.

This is the only fragment of the whole novel that I would subscribe to in talking about myself: the acknowledgment of my excesses. Otherwise, neither the character of the mother (despite certain vague echoes) nor of the father (an amalgam of bits borrowed from a number of models) resembles my mother or my father, nor was my childhood as claustrophobic as the one described in the book.

I never thought that any kind of connection could be

drawn, but clearly I was wrong, for no matter what the characters are like and no matter how different the story is from ours, in some way it portrayed *us*.

I didn't have him in my sights. But it had the same effect on my father as if I had.

And I wasn't unhappy about it.

I discovered that I had a weapon, and I used it.

The first time I consciously availed myself of our problem was in a long story that I wrote for a contest. Under pressure to make the deadline, and afraid that I wouldn't be able to get a handle on someone else's story in time, I resorted to a subject I could identify with immediately: a father, a young son, and the triangulation of feelings when there's dissatisfaction on both sides and one slight leads to another. I chose an isolated and oppressive setting, drastically shortened the time in which the story takes place to ratchet up the intensity, made the narrator take the boy's side, devised an ending that was theatrical, violent, and unmistakable in its implications, and threw myself gleefully into the writing, swept away by an unfamiliar fury that even led me to scatter clues through the story that my father and his circle would recognize without much effort.

Naturally, there were consequences. A while after it was published and my father had read it, he called one day, and in response to his question about how the new book was coming, I confessed that I was stuck. His answer was, "Stuck? Nonsense. Write about a cruel father and his miserable son."

What heightened rather more than briefly the guilt this ironic commentary intended to spark was that—though he didn't know it—the novel I was writing at the time had grown out of that story and was therefore destined to touch on the same subject.

The novel, of course, was more complex than the story,

less reliant on insinuation and the careful employment of verb tenses, and more open to digression and a full exploration of the themes. It, too, alternated between two timelines: a recent past that constituted the novel's present, and a distant, remembered past that functioned as a traumatic explication of the former.

The unresolved conflict that cast a shadow over my narrator's present was a drama along the same lines as the one I'd presented in the story, an anticipated tragedy that, when it arrives, exposes the guilty parties. The victim was once again a boy, and those responsible for his fate were once again members of his own family: a father unable to act the part and deflect the looming threat, and the father's wife, trigger of the danger, the instigator. The narrator, like the narrator of the story, participates in the events as an observer, but unlike the narrator in the story—where the action takes place over the course of a weekend—he might have intervened if he chose, which makes his moral position more ambiguous. The reasons he doesn't intervene—his extenuating circumstances—are his youth at the time of the remembered events and his close relationship to the other three protagonists (son of the instigator, son of the passive father, and half brother of the victim of the injustice described). The simple decision to make the narrator the half brother of the victim allowed me to cast him as a judge of the sins of their common father, much sterner and less prey to charges of Manichaeism than he might have been had he served directly as the victim.

The novel's other story line, the present-day plot, touched on subjects as varied as love, betrayal, and resistance to assume the responsibilities of adulthood, and there's no need to summarize it here; suffice it to say that some of the trappings coincided with those of my own life: the narrator's age, place of origin, social class, and schooling were similar to mine. Also,

I scattered so many private references and secret winks for the benefit of those who, like my father, were capable of unearthing them that before I sent the final version to the publisher, I was attacked by remorse and spent a few days deleting or softening the most costly, the crudest, those clothed in the weakest metaphors, those that most transparently betrayed their autobiographical roots, those that gave me the most pleasure to write.

And yet it's not entirely true, as I suggest in the lines quoted on the first page of this book, that in the novel I killed my father. In the course of the writing, I made the father of the protagonist die for structural reasons, but he wasn't my father; he didn't even resemble him. Any connection had to be sought elsewhere. Once the plot was established, I loaned the fictional character some traits of my father's, through which I sought to direct his attention to the conflict of loyalties played out in the novel, and to the extent that this really was a distorted version of the conflict between us, my intent was to show him something like an image projected on a river, a shadow distorted by ripples of water in motion, an image that hints but doesn't dictate and could therefore be of anyone. Not a portrait or a true mirror able to return to him a clear image of himself, but rather a cluster of echoes that harked back not only to our story but also to the story of my mother and her father, so similar in many ways to ours that it may have fed my fears, leading to errors of judgment and unfair comparisons that caused me to be too hard on him.

Triangulation, concealment, exaggeration, cross–contamination . . . The fact is that I used my father. The substance of the book grew out of our deepest misunderstandings; I had him in mind in many passages; and I'd hate it if my memory of him should be tainted now in unjust retribution.

Fiction, even when it's inspired by reality, obeys its own

rules. It alters reality by pursuing different ends than those of fidelity to the truth. The fathers in my novels weren't mine, and I want the father I write about here to be who he was to me.

I want to strip him of accretions.

I gave my two novels everything I had, I poured myself into them, and I'm still feeling the consequences today; I write against that.

Did he know it?

He must have known, I'm sure, that the intensity of what we shared at the end of his life would inspire me. When— on our last trip, chasing a hope that we knew was remote— I accompanied him on consecutive afternoons to the derelict hospital of an African island, he allowed himself to direct my gaze to our surroundings and even to give me an idea or two. He was already seeing himself from the outside, a dying hero from a Conrad novel. *Take a good look at all of this,* he advised me, *because later you'll be able to use it.*

He probably knew I would want to make up for the times I had used him for my own ends.

But did he guess that there would be no masks, that it wouldn't be fiction I would write this time?

In his excessive reserve, he would have recoiled at the idea, but as I've said, he changed so much toward the end that I can't be sure. I suppose that when you face death, a new kind of logic takes over. The performance has ended. Your immortality is in the hands of others, and almost anything can be forgiven.

It's odd, in any case, that in my previous books I was able to explore in depth thoughts that he inspired, and that now, face-to-face with him, I miss fiction.

✳

From 1984 on, our lives hardly change. My father has become a problem for me. One among others. My mother weighs on me, for example. I feel the weight of her loneliness and my loneliness with her. But even here he's somehow implicated. It's his absence that heightens the loneliness.

After a very difficult year in which we go into debt and survive thanks to the help of my grandfather, between 1984 and 1990 my mother embarks on a new period of prosperity. Now she works in publicity, and again we spend without a thought for the future.

Between 1984 and 1990, I finish school and start college.

Between 1984 and 1990, I keep a list of the women I've slept with.

Between 1984 and 1990, I discover a love of late nights and I go out to bars where I meet other noctambulists like me.

Between 1984 and 1990, I not only read and write: by now I'm dreaming about becoming a writer. My father observes from a distance. He doesn't show much interest, and when he does, I can't tell from his tone, part incredulous and part skeptical, whether he approves or whether—as it occasionally seems—he's trying to discourage me. Nevertheless, when in '88 I publish my first article, he carries the clipping around in his bag for days to show to his friends.

Between 1984 and 1990, he continues to fix up places with the friend he met in Brazil. In personal matters, after endless bargaining, each of them has ceded enough to put their relationship on a solid footing.

Between 1984 and 1990, he gets past the worst of his crisis and returns tenaciously to painting after four years in which a new generation of artists has established itself. He shows in less prestigious galleries; he tries to find a niche for himself. He doesn't always manage to attract the notice of the influence peddlers, the speculators in early fame, but he regains the respect of his fellow painters. He shows in 1984, in 1986, and again in 1987. These are the years that a critic of his work will describe as his time in the desert. It's a titanic struggle, in which he's obliged not only to see himself in the mirror of others with less talent but also to wrestle with many people's lack of faith.

Between 1984 and 1990, the life he leads with the friend he met in Brazil settles into a pattern. They keep a place in Madrid, one that changes for the better as their joint business ventures prosper. They spend two months of the summer— sometimes three—at the beach and almost every winter weekend in the country. It's a bourgeois existence that pleases them both, but my father must escape it to immerse himself in painting. It's hard for him to adapt to such a conventional schedule. Not just where vacations are concerned, but also in daily life.

Between 1984 and 1990, I go out often with my mother. Her friends are writers, filmmakers, journalists; among them there are plenty of bon vivants and social butterflies. I accompany her to parties and book launches; we host dinners at home.

Between 1984 and 1990, I become aware of the fragile ground on which my mother and I tread, the little we're left with if she takes a false step, but since she isn't faltering now, I enjoy our run of good luck. I reign supreme. Everything around me is lax. I take what I want of what I'm offered. The only person I must yield to is my father, and only where he's concerned do I feel that I'm deprived of anything.

Between 1984 and 1990, I become increasingly convinced that my needs are of secondary importance to my father, as am I myself.

Between 1984 and 1990, there are three men in addition to my father whom I see often enough to count as influences, after whom I model myself. My father isn't the one in the ascendant, but he has the power to unman me with his aloofness, to drive me mad with his deficiencies.

And everything happens very quickly. I'm trying to reproduce that quickness now, in memory, aware that no single occurrence that I've described will explain who I am. Everything is insufficient or, at best, misleading.

In 1984, on the answering machine at the house my father shares with the friend he met in Brazil, I record the sound of a toilet flushing. I schedule an automated wake-up call for the middle of the night. In 1984 we fabricate a cast for my mother before the visit of a suitor whom she—as an excuse for not taking a trip with him—has told that she's broken her leg. In 1984 I ask one of my mother's friends to review a show of my father's.

In 1985 I spend two weeks with my father and the friend he met in Brazil, our only vacation together. This is the summer that people start to talk about AIDS, and when we get back, I come down with a summer flu that I become convinced is a symptom of the disease. My father visits me one afternoon and puts an end to my delusions by taking me for some tests. That same summer, on the beach, I win his startled respect when I hook up with the one girl who catches his eye. What I don't tell him is that both times we watched the sun come up together, all we did was make out.

In 1985 my cat has to be put to sleep. It's my father who takes care of it.

In 1985 we put my mother's place up for sale in order to move downtown. Afraid that we'll squander the money, my father won't help us in the search for a new apartment until the operation is irreversible, and feeling overwhelmed, I demand his help.

In 1986 there's the NATO referendum, and my mother, my father, and I go to vote at the polling place in our old neighborhood, where my father is still registered. He does it grudgingly, as if it pains him to accompany my mother and me.

In 1986 my grandfather on my father's side dies without knowing that my parents have been separated for ten years or being aware of the existence of the friend my father met in Brazil.

In 1986, the day before my father leaves for Warsaw for an artists' conference in Eastern Europe, he informs us that in his absence my mother will receive a petition for divorce. We let him know that we're unhappy that he's chosen to do it this way rather than opting for a consensual divorce, and after my mother informs him that given the circumstances, she won't make it easy for him, I walk him to the Metro in silence. My mother's resolve lasts scarcely a few weeks. After discussing it with me, she calls a lawyer and gives him the go-ahead to take my father for all she can get, but when we have my father on the ropes, we relent. Before this, I write him a letter that the friend he met in Brazil intercepts and that earns me her deepest hostility, in which, with a temerity that ashames me now, I ask him not to marry her.

In 1987, when I happen to be in my father's neighborhood with a friend who's an aspiring painter, I stop by his place to ask him to show us his paintings. No one answers the buzzer, but just as I'm about to give up, he comes walking down the street with the friend he met in Brazil. They're dressed up; he's nervous and she's beaming. I immediately guess that they've gotten married, which he confirms days later.

In 1987 I take my college entrance exam, and in the fall I begin my degree in philosophy. My father doesn't hide his surprise when I tell him and asks how I plan to make a living.

In 1987 I have a girlfriend and she's a writer. She's older than I am and pretty wild, which means that neither my mother nor my father likes her, and although my mother pretends otherwise, my father doesn't bother. During Easter, when the friend he met in Brazil is out of town, he invites my girlfriend and me to spend a few days with him in his country house. He makes fun of everything she says, sets traps for her, is condescending to me, and tells unflattering stories about when I was little. At some point I get the sense that he's competing with me.

In 1987 my father and the friend he met in Brazil buy a place together and for the first time both of their names are on the title. My father explains that neither I nor her children will be given the keys, and he promises that everyone will be treated equally. In the same conversation he tells me that they're going to draw up a document in which both of them will agree which household items, paintings, and furniture belong to each. When he gives it to me weeks later, I discover that what was hers is still hers and the only things that will now be shared are his.

In 1988 I spend two months in London, staying with an old girlfriend of his. I'm there to learn English, but all I do is sit at a library, where I read the *Iliad* and the *Odyssey* in Spanish and try in vain to write.

In 1988 my dog has to be put to sleep. Again it's my father who takes care of it, though this time my mother and I are with him.

In 1988 my writer girlfriend cheats on me with a friend of my mother's whom we put up when he comes to Madrid, and months later she leaves me to go to America with an ex-boyfriend. I find out that my father, who got the news from me, has told the whole story to some friends, and when I get upset, he defends himself by attacking her so harshly that I'm deeply offended and abandon him in the middle of the street.

In 1989 he presents me with a painting from a recent exhibition, giving it to me behind the back of the friend he met in Brazil.

In 1989 I ask him to teach me to drive. He gives me one lesson, and days later, explaining why he can't give me more, he says that the friend he met in Brazil has told him that it could be bad for the car.

In 1989, during the summer, while my father and the friend he met in Brazil are away, her son moves into their place. When my father finds this out from me, he sends me the keys and asks me to make an appearance there. Days later, when he gets back, he tells me that he's changed the lock and I don't need to return the keys. He assures me that there will be no more unequal treatment.

In 1990 my mother leaves the publicity agency where she's worked since 1984 and opens a graphic design studio.

In 1990 the friend my father met in Brazil goes away on a trip and I see my father a number of times. One afternoon I introduce him to a friend I've fooled around with a time or two and whom I've tried to steer in his direction. Shortly afterward my friend tells me that they're having a clandestine affair, and a few days later, in need of an alibi, it's my father who brings me up to date. The friend he met in Brazil suspects, and he's given me as the unlikely excuse for his constant absences. At one point he asks me to call her and confirm that he's with me; at another point it's she who calls in tears to try to get information out of me. Meanwhile, when these difficulties cause the relationship to languish, one night I run into my father's lover and we end up in bed. I can't relax, I'm beset by a kind of vague remorse, but I let her fellate me and in the morning I penetrate her briefly.

In 1990 I travel to Russia by train. When I return by plane, my mother and my father are waiting for me at the airport. My mother is eager to see me, and my father can't wait to hear what I have to tell. That same evening, back at home, I take a phone call in front of both of them from a Russian woman, and my father makes fun of me when he hears me call her "love."

From 1984 to 1990 and for years to come, the feelings are all the same; nothing changes.

I live with my mother. I see her morning, noon, and night. She's the one who pays for my education, who clothes me, feeds me. She's the one who notices when I lack something, who comes up with solutions and tries to grant my wishes. She's the one who teaches me how to behave in public, who sets me on the right path, who convinces me otherwise when I announce that I don't want to go to college. Very little that happens to me goes unnoticed by her. She's the one who straightens me out, who rallies me when I need it, and I do the same for her when I can. We face setbacks together, without help. My father isn't around; my father is an intermittent presence. My father creates capsules of time outside of daily life. If I manage to get past his defenses, I can share my worries with him, but without his knowing what my life is really like and without the fortification of material assistance, his advice is out of place, inadequate. I don't even grant him the authority to offer it to me in the first place. Most of the time I don't ask for it. I keep him at arm's length.

Bitterness and resentment plague me constantly. What do I blame him for? For everything. For not seeing me enough, not calling enough, not remembering my birthday, not giving me presents, for vanishing when he knows that my mother and I are in trouble, for spending the summers away and traveling when I don't get to, for failing to keep his promises, for believing that he has more cause for complaint than I do, for thinking that this excuses him, for settling, for presuming that I should accept his capitulation, for seeing me in secret, for giving me things in secret, for giving me money in secret, for thinking that his love is enough, for removing himself from the picture, for delegating everything that concerns me to my mother, for not setting himself up as an alternative to her, for giving me no option, for letting my mother be the sole center of my little life.

Though he does make some effort. Impulsive efforts that he almost always abandons. He's aware of the problem between us and he's jealous of the preference I show for my mother, but he isn't able to put things right. The same old strategies don't work anymore. He tries to have me come and visit him, but I feel strange at his house. He tries to have me spend the occasional weekend with him in the country, but it's the same there. In both places, not only am I conscious that my presence is an inconvenience for the friend he met in Brazil, and not only are restrictions imposed on me that don't apply to her children and that he doesn't protest, but in addition I sense an underlying tension that makes it even more difficult for me to fit in. At home, with my mother, I'm independent, almost an adult. My mother counts on me, relies on me for almost everything, and I assume responsibilities, look out for our mutual interests, and, as a result, enjoy a certain standing. As far as my father is concerned, though, I'm still a child. He hasn't watched me grow up, he casts around for the right tone to take with me, and the friend he met in Brazil is no help. Any difference of opinion or complaint that I voice, no matter how fair, is easier to deflect if it can be chalked up to immaturity. Immaturity and my mother's influence. This is the equation to which I see myself constantly reduced. So I ignore his invitations, which anyway aren't as frequent as they should be.

In eighteen years we spend only part of a summer together: the two weeks previously mentioned, which he asks me to book months in advance. Those two weeks aside, we spend no more than ten nights under the same roof. Gone are the days when he picked me up from school. Now our life is reduced to a lunch or two a month. Except for the dinners he has with friends after his openings, I don't know what he's like at an evening meal. I haven't seen him drunk. Or first thing in the morning. We meet when the day has already begun. He usually chooses Tuesdays because that's when he meets some of his painter friends for drinks. He picks me up and we go to a neighborhood restaurant. Then he naps in a chair at my apartment, with the TV on, and leaves around five. We never have dinner. At most, if we're on very good terms, we spend part of the evening together. Once or twice— hardly ever—we go to the movies. Once or twice—if it's been a long time since we've seen each other—I go out for drinks with him and his friends.

In many ways we're two strangers. He doesn't know me outside of our contrived lunch dates, and I have a very limited idea of his life. I get tiny snatches of it, isolated instants over a plate of food. I don't know what he does for fun. I don't know what he's like at home before he goes to bed, what he does, whether he reads or watches television. I don't know who most of his new friends are, what his plans are until they aren't plans anymore but realities. I don't know anything about him, and I have to fill in the gaps with stolen glimpses. Because of this, and because I often have the feeling that he hides information from me so as not to hurt me, I don't miss a thing when we're together. I'm alert to body language, to a hand reaching too often for the bread, to a clearing of the throat, to lips pasted together. I retain everything he says, and it's easy for me to detect contradictions.

And then, too, there are long stretches during which no news is exchanged, during which we don't call each other. It happens when I'm nursing a grudge about something and he—rather than confronting me, getting me to talk, defending himself—beats a retreat. He doesn't call me and I don't call him. And so on, until one of us relents and takes the first step. Usually, he's the one. The phone rings and I hear his voice. The tension is palpable. It's clear that there are a thousand other things he'd rather be doing, clear that he has no intention of trying to address the cause of our impasse, that he intends to leave things as they are, not advance them, only resume the interrupted status quo, clear that he's afraid of my reaction, aware that only the smallest recrimination, the tiniest sarcastic remark would be enough to prompt a new outburst and a new standoff.

We never manage to get past the problem between us. It's always there beneath the surface. Catastrophe looms. It's not relaxing for us to be together. We study each other, measure our words, speak in generalities, talk about the weather, talk about family, talk about our work, talk about politics, and almost never talk about ourselves, he striving to keep the conversation on neutral ground, and I tongue-tied, testing ways to obliquely introduce my demands. Most of the time I don't address them head-on. When I do, he lets a second or two go by, his displeasure evident in the longer silence, in his change of expression, and if I persist, there might be a confrontation. Confrontations are always the same: after my initial complaint, he parries with an excuse, I ratchet up the pressure, he defends himself heatedly, and I respond in kind until it becomes impossible to take things any further without making a scene and we're silent for the rest of the meal. When we leave the restaurant, either each of us goes his own way, or, if I'm feeling remorseful, I walk him to the Metro trying to pretend that nothing has happened.

And we part. Upset, both of us. I let off steam at home and he probably works out his frustration by subjecting the friend he met in Brazil to an afternoon of ill humor. Though sometimes he must not be able to avoid talking, it's hard for me to imagine that he tells her everything; he can't want to make trouble. A vicious circle—my father, the friend he met in Brazil, and me; the grudges of each constantly feeding off those of the others.

After a fight, I know that it's on his mind for days, but I have no idea to what extent it affects his life. I suffer the effects hugely. I work myself up; I egg myself on. Alone, I envision revenge; when I'm out, I'm carried away by euphoria. I talk more than ever, I drink more than ever, I'm always the last to leave, I contrast myself to him in the arrogance of my youth. But if I feel vulnerable, at a loss, I do none of this, instead lapsing into a state of tortured apathy; sometimes I cry. Or I alternate between the two states, euphoria and prostration. Or I throw myself into writing as if I'm competing with him in a stupid race.

The rope is always taut. There's never a slackening of tension. He suffers and I suffer, but we can't let it snap, can't do without each other.

More often than I should, I think about his death. I wonder whether anything will have changed by then. I wonder whether he'll be capable for once of acting according to the convention between fathers and sons. What will happen to his things? What will happen to his paintings? If he can't do right by me while he's alive, he won't do right by me in death either. And I get angry. Especially because I know that he's simply blind to the risks. He takes it for granted that everything will turn out right without any effort on his part. I get angry because he doesn't realize that if, as he argues, his failure to comply with his paternal responsibilities has some unfathomable cause rather than being due to neglect or disregard, he should at least make sure that what he has to leave—his paintings, his belongings—will reach my hands.

He says that the friend he met in Brazil covers most of their common expenses, but I do the math and it seems to me that ever since he gave up renovation work, he makes enough from painting to support himself.

He says that the friend he met in Brazil put down more money on the house where they live, but I include as part of his contribution all the unpaid work he's done for her and all the sought-after paintings by other artists that he's sold, paintings that back in the day he was savvy enough to buy or that were given to him by their more established creators.

He says that the friend he met in Brazil is generous with him, but I'm convinced that while his own money is frittered away on their daily necessities, she's saving for herself. If the family car breaks down, it's he who buys the next one. If there are repairs to be made at home, he pays for them; ditto if they take a trip. As I see it, she squeezes him, controls him, and manipulates him, but my father doesn't realize it, and what's worse, since he's oblivious to how the money is used, he feels permanently in debt. It doesn't surprise him, or at least he doesn't show it, that she makes him sign papers. It doesn't surprise him, or at least he doesn't show it, that they're always short of cash.

All of this, accurate or not, runs repeatedly through my head when I'm frustrated with him; and because it's my view of things and not his, if at any point I make some mention of it, he gets irritated, cuts short the conversation, and obliquely accuses me of self-interest. What he refuses to see is that what I want is for him to stop feeling indebted, because it's his indebtedness that comes between us. What he refuses to see is that even when I talk about money, what I'm really talking about is feelings. What he refuses to see is that I need to have proof that I matter to him.

I don't trust anything, and that's also part of the problem between us.

There's only one area, in fact, in which there is no risk of conflict: I'm proud that he's a painter; I admire his work. Where it's concerned, I'm always ready for a temporary truce. He knows this and appreciates it, and in his own way he takes advantage of it. If he has a show coming up and we're not on terrible terms, he often asks me to come to his studio. He suggests it timidly, but he makes it plain that I'll be letting him down if I don't come. It's not a tactic to bring us together; I think he really does value my judgment. I deduce this from the unhurried way he shows me the paintings, waiting silently to hear what I have to say, taking his time to respond. It's a tradition that dates back to his crisis, when I insisted that he return to painting and I even permitted myself to be tough on the initial results. I'm careful, I never offer a solely negative opinion, but I don't hide what I think.

One afternoon I mention that almost all his paintings repeat the same compositional scheme, with a figurative motif—usually a photograph taken from a magazine, distorted and painted over—around which the space of the painting arranges itself. I refer to it in passing, but it makes an impression, since the next few times he makes joking reference to the *figurita central*, as I innocently called it, and some time later his painting evolves toward a fractioning of the canvas that, by multiplying the *centers*, puts an end to the very notion of center.

I like it that he's a painter. I admire him, I visit his studio, I tell him what I think about his paintings, I help him maneuver the biggest ones out the window when the handler from the gallery comes for them, but I'm not entirely impartial either. It's in my interest to foster that complicity. I sense that he doesn't have it with the friend he met in Brazil, and I don't want to fail him as I imagine that she fails him.

And meanwhile, life goes on.

In 1991 I spend two weeks in Mexico with a friend who's attending a writers' conference.

In 1991 I steal books from bookstores.

In 1991 I dress in vintage blazers and I almost always wear a scarf knotted around my neck, something that he misses no chance to make sly fun of when he sees me.

In 1991 I flirt with a waitress at one of the late-night bars where I'm a regular, but it's another waitress—mistakenly believing herself to be the object of my attentions—with whom I end up in bed.

In 1991 I hardly ever go to class, and when I do, I show up late, sometimes without having slept, often hungover, often feeling dirty.

Today, as I write this in the late spring of 2008, I ask myself whether I've properly gauged the play of memories with which I aspire to approach an impossible objectivity. My feelings aren't always the same, times change, and occasionally I notice that I'm leaving something out. I've talked, for example, about my father's family, but I realize that I haven't described him, that I've hardly said anything about what he was like.

He wore glasses and was a skinny boy who stood out in the rough squalor of the schools of postwar Madrid. He wasn't fearful, but he preferred his own realms: his grandparents' house in the summer, his girl cousins on his mother's side of the family, the French edition of *Elle*, to which his older sister subscribed and which, in addition to the usual fashion stories, ran reviews of books, music, and art. Once, talking to me in the hospital about those days, he said that he remembered himself as always being sad.

"After your mother died?" I asked.

"Always."

Adolescence strengthened his body, and in his youth, it was his unexpected beauty, the effect it had on women, as well as the decision to be an artist, that gave him confidence. He became a painter, lived in different places, but the boy in glasses crouched inside of him and occasionally returned to seize control, paralyzing him whenever life most resembled a schoolyard.

He kept a diary of trivial events—what he had done, whom he had seen, his progress on his current painting—recorded in brief entries and occasionally shaded with faint strokes that provided glimpses of his state of mind. Often he crossed out several days in a row and wrote *fight* or *pissed*. It was as far as he would let himself go, on the off chance that eyes other than his might read what he had written. The fights were usually with the friend he met in Brazil, but also with me.

He had a tendency to gain weight. He liked food and drink, and because he was vain, he was permanently dissatisfied with his weight. He was a competent cook, but he was just as happy to eat the worst junk, with which he soothed the anxieties that gnawed at him.

He had a weakness for fried food and for anything in béchamel sauce; he preferred meat to fish, but he had a great fondness for cod and anchovies and also eggplant; he liked cured meats, pasta, meat loaf, meatballs; he liked cabbage, beets, tuna, liver with onions; he didn't care for any other kind of offal and he didn't much like salads, most seafood or shellfish, or any raw fish. He liked Chinese food and Indian food and Mexican food and hamburgers and sausages. He liked wine and beer.

Almost every evening he had a drink, but as far as I know, he didn't favor a particular liquor. He chose based on what was available and on the fluctuation of his tastes. Rum, whiskey, gin, bourbon . . .

He smoked for a while, but he was one of those smokers who is always trying to quit, and finally he did quit.

He was humble with the meek and contemptuous with the arrogant, but humility and contempt alike were expressed from the grips of a nervous agitation, so that neither was perceived by its recipients with total clarity, blurred by the haste with which he hid himself or dealt a blow.

He was impatient and, as a result, often committed injustices. In speaking to a waiter or concluding a conversation.

He could tell a good jacket or a good shirt when he saw one, and he knew the ways of high society, having grown up with them, but his pride and his masculinity barred him from pretending to be something he wasn't. Tending to a pair of handmade shoes or a bespoke suit with the calculated care of someone who can't replace them as frequently as he'd like, taking refuge in appearances, being frugal to strategic effect, donning some disguise would have run counter to his convictions and his character.

In the fifties he adopted the tailored jacket typical of intellectuals and artists of the period, worn with a turtleneck sweater or a V-neck sweater without a tie; in the sixties, this look was replaced by blazers and jeans, often worn with boots; at the beginning of the seventies he let his hair grow, wore looser clothes, experimented with extravagant accessories and pendants; in the eighties the colors got brighter . . . Then the years began to pass more slowly; tones changed; fabrics changed. Ever since I can remember, he always owned at least one suit, but his frequent weight swings meant that he couldn't wear it for long. When he had to dress up, he just added a jacket and a tie to jeans. If solemnity was required, the jacket would be classic, wool or silk, but if the occasion permitted—say, one of his own openings—he was bolder and dug out some gaudy specimen from his collection of tacky ties bought in New York. In winter he wore a military or Barbour jacket; he liked it to have inside pockets, zippered if possible. He wore unremarkable shoes, loafers with rubber soles or moccasins. He kept his keys on a carabiner, hanging from a belt loop, and he carried shoulder bags. In the seventies and eighties they were made of brown leather, which he brushed until it shone, and beginning in the nineties, they were of black fabric, matching the dark clothes he had begun to wear not so much according to the dictates of fashion, but in order to hide his girth. Outside, he walked with a hand on his bag to protect it. At my apartment and his, he always left it at his feet so that it would be nearby whenever he might need it. In it he kept his wallet, an agenda, the case and chamois cloth for his glasses, a notebook, tissues . . .

He hated any kind of distinguishing feature denoting class or group differences.

.

He liked his comforts. He liked comfortable and well-decorated houses, and he liked pretty things, liked to possess them. He was a fetishist, not a collector; he didn't accumulate. He was attracted to antiques, though he never lost the pop sensibility that made him tolerant of kitsch. He had an eye that could take almost any object out of context and bestow upon it a singularity it had previously lacked. He had no time for the ostentatious or the pretentious, nor did he let himself be seduced by contemporary versions of classic modern furniture. He had a Breuer tube chair, but his was an original. He didn't seek out specific pieces. He preferred serendipitous finds. Actually, his decorating style, with its integration of diverse elements, was reminiscent of his later paintings. He was always seeing things from a new angle, discovering an unexpected side—of an Elizabethan desk, a religious carving, the vertebra of a whale, a Japanese engraving, a polka-dotted sixties lounge chair, some souvenir . . . He bought English and American design magazines, and every Sunday morning at eight he visited the Rastro in search of bargains. His greatest domestic sins were committed when he let himself be carried away by whims at antique shops or auction halls, and his trips almost always yielded some piece that for a while sat enthroned in a prominent spot in his house.

.

He was curious about almost everything.

.

He was a cultured man, it goes without saying.

.

When he was young, and into his thirties, he was a conscientious and up-to-the-minute reader of fiction and poetry and essays, but little by little he was overcome by laziness and became more of a dilettante, fussier. He asked me to recommend books for him, lend them to him, but since he almost never actually read them and was slow to return them, I seldom did.

·

He liked Cioran.

·

He liked Madrid, the city where he was born, and he liked to read books about it.

·

He had seen good American and European postwar films, Bergman, nouvelle vague, Italian neorrealism, but as the years went by—and this was true for him with fiction as well—he gradually developed a kind of distaste for plots that were too involved, especially those dense with tangled sentiment.

·

He preferred humor. He liked Buster Keaton, he liked Charlot, he liked the Marx Brothers, he liked Cantinflas, he liked Tati, he liked Jerry Lewis, he liked Woody Allen, he liked Benny Hill, he liked Mr. Bean, he liked Tip y Coll, he liked Faemino y Cansado.

·

His friends say that he was a good correspondent, that his letters were witty and amusing. And yet when he had to write about painting, he was overcome by modesty. It wasn't his thing to play the expert, pontificate.

·

Like so many men of his generation, he was something of an erotomaniac. For a while he collected old erotic postcards, and his library never lacked for good photography collections of contemporary nudes. On my first trip to Paris on my own, when I was seventeen, I bought him a book of 1890s erotic daguerrotypes, titled—I believe—*Kaleidoscope*.

In addition to Spanish, he spoke English and French. Not fluently, for he had hardly studied them, but confidently—well enough to read and carry on a conversation.

Beginning with his first show in 1959, he moved from abstract expressionism through informalism, through the so-called new figurative art, through pop art. In his best work, over the last twenty years, he favored abstraction, incorporating into it written words and small figurative elements that, following a certain initial lyricism, gradually became part of an increasingly sharp play of planes. The expressionist inheritance of his paintings can be seen in their gesturalism, and as a result, they never seemed especially labored. And yet that was what he was: laborious. He had excessive facility, and he struggled against it with fierce tenacity. On his lips, the worst criticism he could muster for one of his own works was *gemlike*. His understanding of painting was too deep to allow him to settle for some decorative or complacent attempt that didn't reflect the tension that arises from true works of art. Alone in front of the canvas, he thought not about his rivals, but about his masters. He yearned for simplicity (sometimes simple complication), but he arrived at it by tortuous paths. Hidden beneath many of his paintings, under layers of paint, are several earlier paintings. In general, when a painting didn't come out right the first time—his greatest joy—he circled it, closing in on it obsessively until it did come out right. Hardly ever was he able to abandon a painting.

After his return to painting in the mid-eighties, he usually worked in the mornings. He painted on the floor, with acrylics. Listening to music. I never saw him at these moments, but I understand that he prowled around for a while preparing his materials, studying the canvas, and that once he had begun, he alternated between a deep absorption in his task and frequent pauses during which he sat and contemplated the painting. If he got stuck, the pause was longer, and he turned to something else for a breath of fresh air. In recent years he cut pictures out of the newspaper, pictures that said something to him, pictures of cardinals descending a staircase, of anonymous people, of politicians at their podiums, of animals, and he glued them into a notebook, labeling them with the date.

The floor of his studio was covered in paint spatters, drips in every shape and color, the outlines of pieces of card that he'd painted without worrying about going over the edges with the brush, sticky spots, and heaps of clots where a pot of paint had spilled. From the walls hung pieces of tape that he used to trace straight lines in his paintings, and every object—his tools, of course, but also the radio and the telephone—was covered in splashes of paint.

He was handy, but not meticulous, and like all those who tend toward disorder, he tried to assign each of his possessions a place. In the studio this was clearly impossible, but everywhere else in the house he managed it. Each photograph, each book, each medicine was easy to find. In his bedroom, he was especially pleased with a 1940s dresser in whose many drawers he kept everything from a shoehorn and his headphones to the wristwatches (never expensive, almost always eccentric) that he retired one by one. Until recently, as a final testament to his departure, at my mother's house we kept a drawerful of his X-rays.

He was an iconoclast and he was irritated by commonplaces, but that doesn't mean he rejected the past. It held an attraction for him. I wrote this somewhat unthinkingly, but I realize that it's true. He read history; he had a fondness for the whole genre of biography—memoirs, collections of letters, diaries—and when he traveled or stayed awhile somewhere, he researched it thoroughly. At his country house he spent endless afternoons going through two chests he found in the cellar that were full of the papers of previous inhabitants. Everything merited his interest, from a 1910 boundary dispute to the price of wheat in 1930.

And yet he was terrified by anything that had to do with death, and especially occultism.

He was moderately superstitious and often wore good-luck charms. The final one was a crow's bone that he removed from around his neck after he got sick, concluding that it brought him bad luck.

He liked music of all kinds. African, French chanson, bossa nova, jazz, reggae, salsa, flamenco, classical . . . He bragged jokingly about having danced better to rock and roll than anyone else in Spain, and up until nearly the very end, if he was happy he would get up from the sofa and improvise a few solo steps. He accused me of not knowing how to dance, though the truth is that we were never together on the right occasion, or at least an occasion that wasn't forced.

He was competitive.

Not a day went by when he didn't do the crossword puzzle in the paper, and if someone in his presence hadn't completed a puzzle or was completing it too slowly, he would grab it and finish it himself.

He watched television, enjoyed it, and was irritated by the phoniness of other people's public denial of the habit. He watched it after lunch as he dozed or did other things, and possibly at night.

At cheap restaurants he wiped his glass and silverware with a napkin. He was squeamish. If I touched my shoes or my feet, he scolded me; if I didn't wash my hands before eating, he scolded me; if I touched a bar or strap unnecessarily on public transportation or touched anything on the street, he scolded me. He could be very scathing about it.

He was affectionate. Brusquely affectionate: his hasty pats on the back were intended to cancel out the ease with which he got choked up.

I have to pick up the chronological thread again because otherwise I'm afraid that the distance I feel from the person I used to be will paralyze me and all my efforts will be in vain.

From 1991 to 2002, it's the same feelings all over again, and sometimes worse, the skein of mutual resentment growing tangled.

From 1991 to 2002, I make frequent attempts to absolve and forget, turn over a new leaf, but something always happens to stir everything up again.

From 1991 to 2002, there's an extremely long period during which I'm in serious financial straits, during which I face responsibilities for which I'm not prepared, and the contrast with my father's comfortable life wounds me. From 1990 to 2002, I often feel brushed aside by him, abandoned in my difficulties.

In 1991, after a nearly sold-out show, my father buys me a stereo and heads to Peru and New York for a few months with the friend he met in Brazil. In 1991, when he returns, I tell him over the phone that while he was away, her children moved back into their house, and when I visit later, the friend he met in Brazil lashes out at me. She screams that I have no say there. She screams that the woman is the mistress of the house and she gives the keys to anyone she likes. Her rage grows, the insults mount, and there's a moment when I break down and cry. It bothers me that one of her children witnesses it all, and that after a few weak attempts, my father doesn't stand up for me. For days I don't pick up the phone when he calls, and when we see each other at last, he brings me a set of house keys on a ring to which he's tied a beach stone. Some time later, however, I discover that the friend he met in Brazil has replaced the lock on the door that separates the entryway from the rest of the house. When I point this out to my father, he claims that the door in question is never locked and that he doesn't have a key to it either. When I tell him how absurd that is, he says he doesn't care, that if he ever finds it locked, he'll break it down himself. Soon afterward, he actually does, but the door is repaired and the lock changed.

In 1991 there are a few months when I don't see my father.

In 1991, one morning when I'm especially tired of myself, on my way out of class I notice a girl, in red lipstick and a beige coat, sitting on the stairs, and because of her I become a regular at the university library and cafeteria.

In 1992 I'm living at my mother's with the girl in red lipstick. Tensions arise from our shared living situation; my father observes it all from such a distance that his interventions are worse than useless. He hints that he doesn't like my girlfriend, but he seems to want to please my mother, to take her side this time.

In 1992, one night when I'm passing by my father's house, partly to rattle my girlfriend, who's with me, and partly out of the resentment I always feel, I ring the bell and we run away.

In 1992 my father has a show in New York, and he spends some time there with the friend he met in Brazil.

In 1992, in June, I graduate from college and my mother gives me a year to write.

In 1993 my father loans me the keys to his country house so I can go there with my girlfriend for the weekend. Days after we return, the friend he met in Brazil, from whom my father has vainly tried to hide this, calls to berate me for having been there. This time my father joins in on the other phone when he hears her yelling, argues with her, and threatens to move out if she doesn't give up her obsession with me.

In 1993 I've begun my first book. I write it at night while my girlfriend sleeps in the same room. Each time I finish a story I send it to a writer friend of my mother's for suggestions. In April I win an arts grant after submitting what I've written. It's just one more occurrence, as fortuitous as most of the others that constitute this timeline. I might just as well not mention it or bring up other equally true-to-life events, and the substance of the story would be unchanged.

In 1993, one day at the end of the summer when I call my father at ten-thirty at night, the friend he met in Brazil gives me a nasty scolding for calling so late and hangs up after informing me that he's in the country. I do reach him there, and since he's alone, he invites me to come out for a few days. I arrive the next morning by train, but late that afternoon the friend he met in Brazil appears. She comes stealthily into the house, bursts into the living room where we're watching a movie, and without greeting me or my father, she says to her daughter, who's with her, "I told you he wouldn't waste any time coming here." My father, if he hears this, shows no sign of it. That night I sleep with the daughter in a room open to the living room, she in the bed and I on the floor on the sofa cushions. After the light is turned out, in the half darkness and perfectly conscious of what I'm doing, I get out of my make-shift bed, naked as I am, and go to the kitchen for a glass of water. When I come back, the daughter of the friend my father met in Brazil invites me to climb in next to her. After a second of hesitation, in which I'm tempted to consummate this petty triumph, she thinks better of it and I return to my bed, relieved.

In 1993, in the fall, my father has an opening in Cologne and then he travels around Germany with the friend he met in Brazil.

In 1994 they go to Austria, where he has shows at galleries in Innsbruck and Kufstein.

During one of these trips I risk letting myself into their house with the keys tied to a beach stone that my father gave me a few years before. As I expected, I find the second door locked, and I can get no farther than the entryway. Later, when they're back in Madrid, I try my luck one day when I know they're out to lunch. Since their absence will be brief, I suspect that the friend my father met in Brazil may not have taken precautions, and I'm right. I spend a frenetic half hour inside and emerge with two bottles of wine from the cellar. I do this again a few days later.

That same year, 1994, after finishing my story collection, I send it to an editor chosen because of her friendship with my mother, and the editor soon rejects it with a letter that ends like this: "The same manuscript, on the same subject, once the craft has been learned, might have the potential to become a book." In 1994 my mother's business is in trouble, and we spend months cutting corners to make ends meet, but that night my mother, my girlfriend, and I go out to a restaurant for a consolation dinner. Before we go, I talk to my father on the phone, and he hints that maybe the book is no good and asks whether someone trustworthy has read it. He's at a loss, caught between his realist instincts and his desire to encourage me. For the same reasons he reacts cautiously when a few months later I tell him that another publisher will bring it out in the spring of 1995. He asks me for the manuscript, or I offer it to him; he leafs through it in front of the television and concludes that he'd rather read it after it's published.

That fall of 1994, faced with the prospect of my approaching literary debut, I make up my mind to spend four months in Ireland studying English. I still have half of the money from the arts grant I was awarded the year before, but I need a bit more and I ask my father for it. At first he refuses, saying that he went to London when he was my age and worked as a waiter, but in the end he gives in. After I've been in Ireland for a while, the money runs out, and I call my mother to ask her for an equal sum. I try to reach her at her office, but no one answers, and finally I discover that she has shut down the business and she's out of work. She has no unemployment income, either, because she's been drawing on it for a while.

My return to Madrid in the spring of 1995 is bittersweet. I'm nervous about the book coming out and I'm nervous about my mother's situation.

In May there's a release party for the book. My father, who has just arrived with the friend he met in Brazil from an opening of a show of his work in New York, asks my permission to bring her. The day in question they arrive first thing, but with a discretion that I appreciate, she stays just long enough to wish me luck. That night, after the celebration dinner, my father leaves in a hurry, not staying for drinks. The armistice has lasted just long enough for us to put on a show of fleeting normality. That same year, on New Year's Eve, my mother tries to call my father. It's 11:45, fifteen minutes before the countdown, and I still haven't shown up, though I'd promised to be there hours before. My mother is worried, but the friend my father met in Brazil answers the phone and hangs up when she hears my mother's voice.

The years that follow my return from Ireland are years of insomnia. In 1996 I've begun to write fairly regularly for the papers and I'm making progress on my second book, but my mother is still out of work, and I fear for her future, which is also mine. I help her write CVs, I wait with her for calls that don't come, and at night I go to my room, where my girlfriend is already asleep, and lie there awake. I can't sleep, because I'm walking a very fine line; I can't sleep, because I feel like an impostor. How am I going to support my mother in the future if I don't even know where next month's money is coming from? I feel alone, despite my sleeping girlfriend, to whom I cling in desperation.

Between October 1996 and July 1997, I spend the academic year on a residency in Rome, and I can't stop worrying about my mother. I invite my father to visit, hinting that I hope he comes alone, but either the friend he met in Brazil won't let him come or he's afraid to broach the idea. While I'm gone, my girlfriend continues to live with my mother.

The same unease accompanies me for the next few years—1996, 1997, 1998 . . . years of deprivation, of living close to the bone. The present has become so constricted that only the future matters now. And the future is cause for concern. No one helps us.

In December 1998, a year after my return from Rome, I finish my first novel.

In 1999, in January, my mother's father dies. It's the beginning of a long legal battle between his second family and my mother and her siblings.

In 1999, in November, I win an important prize for the novel. At the press conference, a reporter asks me why I use a second surname, that of my writer grandfather. I answer with the truth, that it's in tribute to my mother, but being inexperienced, I go on longer than I should, and the next day, a newspaper condenses what I've said this way: "Keeping your mother's last name is a great tradition, and in my case it makes sense, because where my upbringing is concerned, I feel I owe more of a debt to her than to my father." In another newspaper I sound harsher and less truthful: "Because of my mother, who has had much more of an influence on me than my father." Remorseful, I call my father, and he assures me that it doesn't matter, but days later I'm angered to learn that his family is hurt. This childish back-and-forth, the inclination to punish him on account of the past for my mother's current difficulties, and my subsequent contrite recognition of the false transposition I've performed also define this stage of our life.

In 1999 my mother has given up on finding a steady job, and her efforts and mine are focused on scraping together enough work so that she doesn't lose her retirement savings. We've also revived an old dream that might secure her future—buying a house in Galicia, where she was born and where it's possible to live cheaply—and to that end we've opened an account where we deposit any extra money that comes in, such as my prize money.

In 1999, when he's halfway through my novel, my father calls me, moved by the passage I quoted earlier in which I describe the narrator's boyhood sense of loneliness. He says "*pobrecito*," in the child's voice he uses when he wants to be affectionate, and I realize that he's reading the whole novel in a personal key. It's possible that an implicit recognition of guilt in response to the passage's overwrought sensitivity has something to do with it, but the point is that because of a book, for the first time he seems to have put himself in my place.

The effects are felt immediately. Though skittish, he's more receptive. While he waits for the stormy weather to lift, he lets me air my worries with scarcely a glimmer of impatience in his gaze. Once or twice he buys me clothes; once or twice he gives me a little money; and once he calls one of his collectors to ask him to give my mother a job as a favor, to no avail.

But that's all.

He has no money, he says. What he makes is hardly enough to cover his share of the maintenance of the house he owns with the friend he met in Brazil.

He wants to see me. He has love to give, but he tries to keep my life from contaminating his. I overwhelm him. He hides when he senses that I'm beset by problems; he turns a deaf ear when I tell him about the endless dispute between my mother and her siblings and her stepmother and children. He's conscious of the parallels, but he doesn't let on.

And he vanishes.

I don't mean to suggest that he doesn't act the part of father. It just isn't consistent. It's been the exception rather than the rule ever since the trouble began between us in my adolescence. The spheres in which he continues to exercise a father's prerogative are as limited as they are symbolic, but occasionally he still does, or I invite him to do so. In the latter case, he goes about it clumsily, whether out of surprise or fear that I'll change my mind, and of course without ever permitting himself to seem recriminatory; when it's the former, he does so jokingly and usually limits himself to the odd comment. For example, he doesn't like it when I go out too much at night, and he often ridicules me for it.

This is a typical phone conversation between us in those days. The phone rings at noon or one; I pick up and hear his voice:

"Did I wake you?" he asks. And then, ironically, "What, were you out last night?"

If I say yes, he says something like "You'll ruin your liver" and proceeds to the object of his call, which is usually to suggest that we get lunch. If I answer that I'm reading, his response is, "You'll wear your eyes out from reading so much." He never asks me where I was the night before, whether he's woken me up, or what I'm reading, if that's what I was doing. In fact, the only answer that receives a non-ironic response is when I tell him that I'm writing, though even then he doesn't ask me what. Probes have been launched to test my mood, a verdict has been reached, and he'd rather not risk a mistake.

These are the lessons he has to offer: "You'll ruin your liver." That's as far as he'll allow himself to go. He doesn't feel authorized to meddle in my life, and my attitude serves as constant corroboration of this. What does he have to say to me, after all? I think and he thinks: after he left home, he relied on my mother for my daily support, and his involvement in everything concerning me, no matter how affectionate or attentive, was cushioned, protected, at a comfortable remove, far from the daily grind of schools and homework, the illnesses and trauma of childhood and adolescence.

These are the lessons he has to offer since before I can remember, and from 1999 on, nothing changes.

In September 2000 my mother and I manage to buy a wreck of a house on the Galician coast. We don't know when we'll be able to rebuild it, but it's an important step in providing for her future, and our pride feeds our hopes. But when I tell my father about it, the speed with which he changes the subject signals to me his wariness and his enduring lack of confidence in us.

In 2001, after a busy year as a result of my prizewinning first novel, I begin a second novel. The prize has meant that between talks and newspaper assignments, I have no lack of work, and as a result, I'm not so oppressed by money worries.

In 2001 I'm awarded a residency in Berlin for the following year. Weeks before I leave, my father tells me that he wants to amend a will he drew up years ago on the initiative of the friend he met in Brazil. He doesn't describe the terms of the earlier will, which I'm hearing about for the first time; he just lets me know that he wants to make me his sole heir, leaving her the use of the house they share. Apparently my tortuous message composed of spoken words, unspoken words, and written words has finally gotten through to him.

In January 2002 I set up house in Berlin. My mother goes to live in Sevilla, where a friend offers her a job, and the girl in red lipstick, my girlfriend—considering that we've been living together for ten years, it's ridiculous that I'm still calling her that—stays in Madrid, tied down by work. Until she joins me six months later, I'm alone in Berlin. For the first time in a long while, stability is visible on the horizon. And I receive visitors, my father first among them. I'm aware that he's had to overcome the opposition of the friend he met in Brazil and I repay him by avoiding any conversation that might cause him to feel questioned. I notice his surprise at this, as well as the fact that as the days go by and I persist in my efforts, he becomes more and more relaxed. This is the closest we've been since those trips we took to London and Amsterdam and Paris twenty years ago. In the mornings I escort him around museums and galleries, and in the afternoons we talk and drink bourbon at home. The only time I betray my intention to avoid bringing up any hardship is one afternoon when he asks for news of my mother and I tell him the truth: things aren't going well in Sevilla, her friend hasn't come through for her, and her life there is lonely and uncomfortable. I also tell him that in a few months we'll have to pay a substantial sum, which we don't have, for some necessary repairs to our building in Madrid. These are two slips, a reflection of other times, but they're the only ones I make, and they don't disturb the atmosphere of understanding. My surprise is great when, ten days after his departure, I receive a letter in which he offers to sell a painting that he bought before his separation from my mother and to give me half the money to defray the aforementioned expenses. In exchange, he asks me to find a buyer.

I return to Madrid with my girlfriend in March 2003 with some savings and three-quarters of a novel. My mother, who left Sevilla a few months ago, is beginning to see a bit of light in the dispute with my grandfather's second family, and she gets some money that she immediately deposits into the account for renovating her future house in Galicia.

In 2004 I finish my novel, and while revising it, I spend three months in Scotland with my girlfriend, as a writer in residence at the University of Aberdeen. We've decided to get married when we return to Madrid; I buy an emerald through a Colombian friend, and while we're away, my parents take it to a jeweler to be set.

The wedding, which is attended by just four family members on each side, is held on the anniversary of the Carnation Revolution. My father, who bought my suit and shirt, is the only one who is visibly moved. He cries during the ceremony and he cries later at a convent where the nuns sing us the Salve Regina.

Slowly, imperceptibly, something has changed between us. I'm still bothered by the same things that have always bothered me, but I've decided not to dwell on them, and the truth is that—though at a snail's pace—he's making an effort too.

I should say a bit more about my work, because it plays a role in our relationship.

In a way, it was a calling pursued behind his back, chosen to distance me from him but not too much, as if I'd asked myself what the profession most similar to his might be and I'd chosen literature as it was the closest at hand. Often I've thought that if I'd seen more of him during my adolescence, when our interests are established, if I'd visited his studio every day, if I'd had the benefit of his encouragement and guidance, if I'd had access to his supplies or his cameras, today I might not be a captive of the word.

My mother's father was a writer, and a rather well-known one, and this, in addition to the fact that I use his last name as well as my father's, is enough to make everyone think it was his example that made me decide to be a writer. I've gotten used to that assumption, but the fact is that my interest in writing had more to do with my painter father.

The world into which I was born was primordially the world of my father. During critical years he was my main aesthetic referent, and it's possible that the visual sense I believe I possess, an intuitive ability to appreciate secret harmonies and to create them myself to the extent of my abilities, is simply the vestige of an apprenticeship prior to the one that made me a writer.

The words were there, in my mother's mouth, shaping reality, capturing life in stories, but I didn't make them wholly my own until I had to use them to define absence, to exercise my memory, seek explanations, construct an alternate personality to my father's, that—being artistic—would at once subsume him and carry with it a necessary dose of rebellion.

I imagine that my father often wondered about my motives, but I suppose he fell prey to the same assumptions as others and took my gradual slide toward literature as proof of my devotion to my mother's family. An homage to the grandfather rather than to the father.

Nothing could be further from the truth.

The comparison was there to be drawn. In the early eighties, when my father was going through the period of depression that distanced him from painting, on sleepless nights I sometimes asked my mother whether he would ever be able to recover and make a name for himself, and she always reassured me that it would be the same for him as it had been for my grandfather, her father, who was in his sixties before he received the honors he had previously been denied. I listened to her, conscious of my grandfather's greater tenacity, of my father's fragility, but despite these reservations, in a comparison of the two of them my father came out on top. My grandfather was too established, too unassailable by now, too self-satisfied, and despite his great learning, too provincial in certain intolerable ways for my inordinately anticonventional taste at the time, whereas my father was a bohemian and had my grandfather beat in eclecticism, rebellion, curiosity, and everything that an adolescent who reads Rimbaud might admire. His lack of money, the absence of the legitimizing umbrella of success didn't undermine his prestige in my eyes, but rather endowed it with an aura of doomed romanticism. Not even the incipient signs of bourgeois lifestyle, when they came, were an obstacle. I explained them away by telling myself that—as in so much else—he was the victim of outside agents. That his true nature was other.

The kind I wanted for myself.

This was at the beginning, of course. Later, it was different.

Later, everything got more complicated. With great sacrifice and hardly any outside encouragement, he devoted himself more assiduously than ever to painting and he began his long fight to recover the ground he'd lost. By dint of hard work, he managed to make a place for himself. Once again he showed in galleries vying to be top-of-the-line, returned to the art fairs, relaunched a quiet international career, and won the occasional prize, while, in the face of his seeming indifference, I finished my studies and did everything I could to become a writer. In the mid-nineties, when I published my first book, the skepticism with which he'd greeted the dawning of my interest in writing was replaced by a surprised recognition of my determination, and later, as I faced up to increasingly tough challenges, by an undisguised pride that at times betrayed glimpses of his enduring dissatisfaction with the path I'd chosen, as well as a pained suspicion—beginning with my first novel—that I was denouncing him in literary form. Nevertheless, he continued to be someone who'd risen from the dead and whose every step required enormous effort, while I was all promise, with everything handed to me on a silver platter. And sometimes, very occasionally, though he immediately made fun of himself for it, he revealed jealousy of the greater media attention that my work received, as well as of the reputation and respect I had begun to gain among people in his world—art critics, for example—without seeing that it was in part the result of social skills that he lacked. I remember one fateful afternoon when he discovered—in a hack-job encyclopedia distributed for free by some newspaper—that while there was a brief biographical entry for me, there was none for him. I could see that he was hurt by this, although his happiness on my behalf was undiminished.

I was pettier. The sadness I felt at seeing the expression on his face, my near-immediate repentance, my regret at his anticipated disappointment, my admiration of his painting, and my sincere belief that he was more deserving—infinitely more deserving—than me, don't excuse the fact that deep down, even if in a muffled and hidden way that I instantly denied to myself, I took some pleasure in his distress.

How vexing for my father, whatever the case. What an uncomfortable fate to have in your own family, in the person of your only child, a disgruntled and suspicious notary who, thinking he knows you, makes an accounting of your weaknesses, your deficiencies, and your broken promises.

But he bore it with dignity, I must say. He permitted himself only the occasional dig. He celebrated my smallest triumphs, and he apparently forgot everything there was to be forgotten: the exaggerations I made, the unconscious blunders in which I discounted his influence on me, and—especially— the misjudgments of him to which some of my literary preoccupations might have given rise. For someone so private, so reserved, this must have been agonizing.

And there we were, each the mirror of the other, practitioners of similar careers, connected by the telephone line. Watching each other from afar, sometimes in anger, sometimes in hopes of reconciliation, sometimes in a precarious state of bliss. There we were, the two of us: he in his studio listening to music while he struggled with a painting, and I in my apartment struggling against myself as I listened to music.

What a trial for my father, despite an underlying current of satisfaction in my successes, to see the uncertainty that so tormented him taking shape in his son's future. What a trial to see everything perpetuate itself, so that in addition to the consequences of having chosen a profession as insecure as painting, he should be further burdened by the consequences of my having chosen a similar profession. How much better it would have been for him if I had embarked on a stable and well-paid career in which personal advancement was based on worth and not on the marketing of a capricious thumbs-up or thumbs-down. A real profession, not the irresponsible pro-longation of childhood that is the nature of artistic endeavors. A profession that would bring me swift returns so that I could overlook his failings.

It's easy to imagine that my father, always worried about money, wouldn't have wanted me to live with the same fear, and not just because he presumed that if I wasn't in need, I would be less likely to blame him for anything. He knew life's ups and downs: he had gone from being a nearly estab-lished artist in his thirties, in the pay of a successful gallery, to a period of drought in which he had to dream up other jobs to survive, and then on to an intrepid rebirth in which, while developing a mature and powerful oeuvre, among the great-est of his generation, and despite his recovered prestige, he hadn't managed to make himself known beyond a small circle of insiders, which translated into respectful but modest re-views each time he had a show, almost no public promotion by important museums, and scanty sales compared with other artists. He knew that in professions like his, either you're a suc-cess or you can't pay the electric bill, and he knew that talent, with few exceptions, isn't what gives you an edge, that it's other qualities, like luck or the ability—not so common among the gifted—not to rouse hatred, prejudice, or envy, which doesn't mean being invisible, but does mean being inoffensive to the egos of those who possess only ego and a tiny bit of power; he knew all this and also how devastating it can feel to be undeservedly brushed aside, and he would have preferred that I not run the risk.

I'm not talking only about material limitations; I'm talking about obstacles to the satisfaction of the artist's exposed vanity, about the recognition, necessary recognition, that my father came close enough to touch and that consequently needled him as late as May 2006, when, in an entry in his diary, he put it this way (I quoted part of this earlier, but I can't resist setting it down in its entirety): "Silence since April 6, and now it's May. I was planning to write something about my state of things but whenever I start, the *why?* gets to me. Now I'm listening to old Gilbert Bécaud songs after slopping paint on an 8×6 canvas that will go to join all the others that I don't know what to do with [. . .]. I have strange feelings in my stomach and my gut and the tiredness has let up a little." He goes on for a brief paragraph talking about me, about the peace—he says—that I've brought him lately, and he continues: "To paint is to make something that didn't exist before. It isn't to erase or to forget; it's to make and to live, so I plan to keep doing it. The paint on this canvas will turn into something that even I can't know; everything will evolve until a certain something appears that demands my recognition and acceptance."

It moves me to imagine my father, sick by now, writing this entry in his diary. Alone in his studio, trying to "make something that didn't exist before," something provocative and suggestive out of some splotches on a canvas. It moves me that he still had the strength not to "erase or to forget," but to "make and to live." What's more, it makes me proud. But what do we do with the doubts? What do we do with the feeling that we've been denied something (or lost it ourselves because in our foolish confidence we let it pass by) that others with less talent enjoy?

Though he may have appreciated my determination and the disdain with which I faced potential failure, my father can't have wanted that fate for me. No father wishes such things on his child: to have no rest, to be always pursuing foolish challenges, to be besieged by thoughts that we don't know how to express any way other than by means of the skill that we've parlayed into a career and that, mistakenly or not, constitutes our way of being in the world.

That's right: I'm no longer talking about recognition, the affront of comparisons, worldly triumphs; I'm talking about that image of my father in his studio on the eve of his death, determined to "keep making." Death and life mingling, as always, but shaded by something that supplants life by merging with it and moreover aspires to triumph over death itself. Something that doesn't allow us to be entirely in any one spot. An itch of unease and doubt and rare hope that in lonely flashes of hard-won inspiration seems to make everything worthwhile. Is it worth tying yourself to a desk, feeling the pull of the rope at your neck each time you venture away from the place where, amid jars of paint, you give your obsessions free rein? How is it possible that a disguise we put on to get through life becomes so confused with life itself that in the end it's one of the main taxes to add or deduct from the final balance as we prepare to leave life behind? And at what point does it begin to hurt when you feel the pull of the rope and you ignore it? At what point do we begin to regret everything that we can no longer fix? Is it always this way?

The worst comes without warning but also without deception. When it comes, we try not to see it, but deep down we know that it's come, it's here, and in the end everything we do to try to escape it just prepares us to accept it (the constant invoking of something, if only to reject it, accustoms us to it, so that by the time it becomes irrevocable, it's the only reality we know). We were no different. When the worst came, none of us who were close to my father wanted to acknowledge it. Friends, acquaintances, everyone abetted us. Somebody had been given the same diagnosis, or knew someone who had been, who had recovered. Even the doctors allowed us to fantasize about the exception, the best possible outcome. It's a parallel reality: willful denial. You hear what the doctors say, you memorize all the possibilities, and what you're left with in the end is the most desirable one. You hear hollow statements like "There are no statistics" or "There's always room for surprise," on the basis of which it's impossible not to speculate, even about a complete recovery. Though you know better, though the look with which these things are said essentially rules it out. There's room for surprise, yes, the look says, but it's best not to expect it. And since you don't want to take their word for it, you consult other doctors, seek out second opinions, recruit anyone who has a doctor friend who might be able to help you, and at the end of the road, you're back where you started, with fewer days left to live intensely.

It's 2005 that's the fateful year.

In 2004 I'm living three hundred miles from Madrid, in a town in the province of Valencia, where, after sitting for her examinations, my wife has gotten a job teaching philosophy. Though both of us try to look on the bright side, it isn't easy: we face several years in limbo until she can enter a transfer lottery. My wife feels guilty, and I'm not always able to hide my frustration.

In 2004 I get angry with my father for the last time, about the painting he offered to sell after visiting me in Berlin. I find a buyer, and he keeps his word and gives me half the money, but it bothers me that he needs to justify it to the friend he met in Brazil by telling her that it's the wedding present he didn't give me when I got married a year ago.

Between 2004 and 2005, I make many calls to the contractor, the architect, and the town hall to finalize the preparations for the rebuilding of the house my mother and I have bought in Galicia as a place for her to live when she retires.

Between 2004 and 2005, I have the feeling that I'm facing changes that will upend my life, and I'm not always optimistic about them. It unsettles me to have left Madrid when my mother is preparing to move away; it unsettles me not to know how long my wife and I will have to live in furnished rental apartments; it unsettles me that my bond with my mother, crucial until now, will become less tight; and it unsettles me that the huge effort I put into my books, the outflow of time and mental energy, isn't be properly rewarded. For the first time, everything seems about to fall into place (my mother's fate is almost resolved, my wife's and mine is taking shape), but I feel tired, and I'm afraid I won't be well-fortified enough for the fast-approaching future.

In February my new novel comes out, and over the next few months I travel frequently to Madrid from my Valencian exile. I make myself available for the few publicity activities; I visit my mother's younger brother, who has cancer; I go out at night; and I travel to Galicia to deal with the contractor.

In April my uncle dies and my father attends the burial with my mother and me. He's affected by my uncle's death, but I also notice his impatience. He isn't at ease, he can't remove himself from the picture, he views any misfortune as a threat.

In May we don't see each other, and at the beginning of

June he calls to say that he's already left the city for the summer and he invites my wife and me to visit. The ritual of past years is repeated. I don't turn him down flat, but both of us know that I won't go. It bothers me that he hasn't let me know in time to give us the chance to meet in Madrid. My summer, shorter than his, is spent in Galicia, in the town where we'll at last begin work on my mother's house in September.

Upon our return everything begins to happen quickly. My wife is back at her school on September 1, and I follow her a month later. Various matters—and a bit of foot-dragging—keep me in Madrid. The novel hasn't done as well as expected, and after the quiet of summer, my hopes give way to discouragement. Except for work assignments, which I complete with more haste than diligence, over the course of the month all I do is flail about, losing myself in the chaos of anxiety, the labyrinth of possibilities. I go out too much at night, and I'm in no mood to shut myself up with another book, something that I inevitably associate with the place where my wife is waiting for me. My wake-up call comes in the form of a stumble at six in the morning in a bar that passes for underground; whether it is or not, what it most resembles is a black hole that you reach already defeated by the responsibilities of the approaching day and from which you emerge hours later with the certainty that once again you've behaved like an idiot. That night I sit down on a sofa near the door to talk to a Russian who says something to me, and as I'm getting up to join the friends I'm with, I trip and split open my chin. To judge by the scar, the cut probably needed stitches. But all I do is cover it with a napkin, and when I leave the place an hour later, I head not to a clinic, but home.

I say that this is my wake-up call because from now on I get hold of myself, and though I'm still in low spirits, I begin preparations for my departure. Among other things, I say goodbye to my father and invite him again to come and visit us. He doesn't reject the offer, but he's so vague about when he might be able to come, without offering any convincing reason, that it's as if he had. Still, we're in a good place. Not just any good place, but one that I expect to be permanent, ever since three years ago in Berlin when I made the decision to wall off the problem between us, remove it from our interactions. Tired of mistrust, I've decided to try giving up my eternal touchiness, which I believe is justified but which dooms us to a difficult relationship, subject to shifts in mood, silences, and mutual trepidation. It's taken me three years to prove to him that our lunches are no longer minefields; with some incredulity he's gotten used to the fact that my hitherto rare visits to his house have become rather more frequent; and just this fall, when he has less than two years left to live but we don't know it yet, I have the feeling that he's finally let down his guard. Since his return to Madrid I've visited him twice, and I've even gone so far as to inform him of my unsettled state. I tell him about staying out too late, and he responds, surprised that I'm confiding in him but scrupulously playing the role that he believes I want him to play. He invokes his own example and assures me that he regrets the time he's wasted in his life. He tells me that he hasn't worked as much as he should have and that the things we pursue in periods of confusion are worthless: vain distractions that sooner or later fade. He tells me that I have talent, a promising career, a wife who supports me, and that it's absurd to lose any more time. All of this he says in a low voice, not so much to prevent the friend he met in Brazil from hearing us as to stress the importance of what he's saying and leave no room for doubt. It's a curious situation, something completely new.

My father—whom I've never allowed into my private life, as punishment for all the times he failed me—is giving me advice and for the first time unabashedly donning the mantle of father. Even better, leery of the authority I've granted him, he's acting more like an occasional confidant than a father. It's the only way. I'm thirty-seven and he's sixty-five, and though his presence in my life may have been constant, it's been so at a comfortable distance, on a very secondary level: he hasn't shared the tribulations my mother has had to endure on my account; he hasn't known the daily uncertainty that children bring; he hasn't seen me suffer or cry; he's had little to do with my hopes or my joys; he doesn't know my friends; he doesn't know me.

It's on my last visit that September—once my late-night drifting has come to an end and neither his advice nor my expressions of regret are necessary any longer, since I've decided to leave, break away, go back to my wife in search of a new routine—when he informs me of the first sign of his illness. He does it so unobtrusively that I hardly notice. I've said that it wasn't like him to clamor for the spotlight, to voice his worries. If this time he does, I can't rule out the possibility that it's his contribution to the new climate of trust, that he's repaying my revelations of the last few days with an equivalent disclosure. Whatever the case, the matter barely occupies the time it takes to be expressed, and it isn't until after I've left Madrid, in our phone conversations at the beginning of October, that it acquires substance in the face of his growing apprehension. His general practitioner has ordered a test, but he has to wait too long for it, the symptoms aren't letting up, and since in the meantime his alarm has grown, he decides to consult a private doctor. By then my involvement is complete. I encourage him to go as soon as possible, and on the day of the appointment, when we talk on the phone, he tells me with ill-disguised distress that they've found a cyst and that, though they've assured him that it's not necessarily malignant, an operation has to be scheduled immediately. I try to calm him with impromptu arguments, but he doesn't listen. He tells me that when it was time to pay the bill, the doctor refused to take any money, claiming that it was because he had no private insurance. That settles it. Each of us is seized by the same dark foreboding; each of us senses it in the other, just as so many times over the course of our lives each has felt what the other felt or thought without having to say a word. We are completely connected, as always, but for the first time, we fear the same thing, hope for the same thing.

Then comes the anxiety, the frenzy of getting the operation to happen quickly, locating the best surgeon, trying to find evidence in the experiences of others to counter our premonitions of doom.

My father is nervous. The friend he met in Brazil is nervous. I'm nervous. Though we don't say so to one another, we know that the worst is here. We're like performers overplaying our roles. My father, the friend he met in Brazil, and me. My father lets down his final defenses and for the first time accepts my help without reservations, even demands it. He's grateful, vulnerable. The friend he met in Brazil gets an inkling that I might be useful in the days to come, and for the first time, she invites me to visit whenever I like. With an attempt at a girlish smile she tells me that the only thing that makes my father forget the wait is my company. I'm presented with the opportunity to prove that my readiness for sacrifice is as great as my past demands, and for the first time, I don't hold back. I don't stop to consider the consequences presented by the future into which we're advancing. I think, of course, and on occasion my thoughts are egotistical, but immediately I rebel and make an effort to cancel out any petty calculation with my actions. I suppose I've speculated so often about this moment that I proceed like someone who's been programmed, like a zombie obeying the commands of his master. I call him every day, and if I'm in Madrid, I visit him in the evenings; I try to entertain him.

The time for the operation arrives, and my father prepares for it with his usual resignation. Earlier, he'd begun gradually to involve me in the doctor appointments leading up to the operation. For some reason, he trusts me more than the friend he met in Brazil. It must be that I retain more information, I explain the things he hasn't understood, I look for solutions, I answer his questions promptly, I'm ready with the most innocuous interpretation. I'm not a caretaker who requires care myself, and he puts his trust in me, responds in kind. The night before the operation, at the hospital, he gives me his bag to keep, invites me to withdraw money from his account if necessary, explains his financial situation, and puts up only a token resistance when I offer to sleep there. Later that same night, as I try to fall asleep in a chair next to his bed, I want to make some pledge in exchange for everything coming out all right, but I can't. I'm afraid to make a promise that I know I won't keep. It's strange. I'm someone who spends his life thinking, trying to keep one step ahead, and I can't allow myself to speculate. Out of fear, but also because I'm still setting my priorities against his. It's my final moment of resistance. A testament to times past.

From now on, without realizing it, I become his father. In the morning I help him shower. He's in good spirits, he wants to do everything right, and my help reinforces his determination. It brings us closer to success. If all is right between us, everything else will be right too. The friend he met in Brazil appears shortly before they come to get him, and I note his impatience with the intrusion of a reality separate from the hospital routine that we've become a part of after our night of initiation.

I think this is the key to everything that happens next. I don't linger on the periphery; I accompany him to the very center of his suffering.

I am his father and he is my son. No one knows what the future holds, but it seems that as long as he's weak and sick, he'll seek my protection. Is he following my lead or am I following his? Is he setting the pace or am I paving the way for his surrender with my own?

He holds my hand until he enters the operating room, and I can't help taking comfort in his deference. While he's inside, my aunt comes, my wife comes, a friend of his comes. My mother doesn't come, so as not to upset the friend my father met in Brazil, but she waits at home for news from us. All the promises I didn't make the night before I make now, walking the hallways, counting the tiles, stepping on only some of them according to a predetermined order.

When the surgeon emerges, I'm the first to spot him. He leads the friend my father met in Brazil and me into his office, and there's no need for him to speak the words he's already speaking. The friend my father met in Brazil is sobbing, and I try to contain myself, but in the end I'm overcome when I ask the practical questions, the questions about time that make doctors most uncomfortable. I feel wrenched apart, outside myself. The person speaking, acting, isn't me. I don't know what goes through my mind. Everything and nothing. When I leave the office, I hug the friend my father met in Brazil and we promise to forget our differences, to pull together from now on. She asks me to keep after her, to constantly be telling her what she should do, and in the first place we agree not to tell my father how little time the doctor says he has left. It's clear that this is all too much for her. "What will become of me?" she asks insistently. She can't hide what for now is her main concern: loneliness.

The worst moment comes that afternoon in the ICU. We enter wearing surgical masks, and my father smiles, flashing a *V* for victory. He doesn't seem to consider that the news might be anything other than good. But before the end of the time we've been allotted, he asks the friend he met in Brazil to leave us alone. I don't know why. He doesn't say anything to me, doesn't ask me anything. I try to act cheerful, like him, but I'm not sure whether I succeed. I start training myself to dole out information in bits. I explain that they've removed the tumor but there are still some nodes that will have to be treated with chemotherapy.

It's what he would want. Or so I believe. His ancestral refusal to verbalize drama allows me to think so. He couldn't handle it.

Over the next few days I continue the tightrope walk of preparing him for what's to come without dashing the hopes that his wide-open eyes plead for, alert to any sign from me. I spend most of my time with him. We've made a schedule to take turns by his side. The friend he met in Brazil is supposed to be with him in the mornings, but it's Christmas, a sister who lives abroad has come to stay, and she begins to cut short her visits. There are even days when she doesn't come. On Christmas Eve she doesn't, and my mother and I have dinner at the hospital.

It's too early to accuse her of desertion, and I play it down when my father expresses his surprise, but I can't help some rejoicing when my lack of faith in her is confirmed yet again. She also mounts strange maneuvers that I notice and that my father must notice too. One morning when we run into each other at the hospital, she invites me to breakfast and tells me that when my father is gone, she'll help me in any way she can. It's clear that gears are turning in her head and she's already contemplating a future without him. She vacillates, caught between two impulses: on the one hand, the need to create a strategy that will require her to become more involved than she is, and on the other, her inability to act selflessly. Probably she's begun to talk to lawyers, or her family is giving her advice, and she gets confused trying to listen to everyone. One minute she's fleeing, gone, and the next she demands unrealistic degrees of responsibility.

One day, all of a sudden, my father asks me for his bag, which I still have in my keeping. One day all of a sudden his dread reappears. One afternoon he's in a state of terror when I come in. He's read a report that the friend he met in Brazil shouldn't have given him, and though the medical jargon prevents him from understanding the full gravity of his case, he's managed to grasp that more organs are affected than we'd let on. I place great stress on the word *microscopic*, which appears in the report, and he calms down, but in his eyes there's a shadow of suspicion, defeat, and desolation that will never go away. On another visit he tells me that the friend he met in Brazil has informed him that he's very sick and he's going to die. As he hopes, I flatly deny that this is true. The following days, he asks me again and sets traps that I don't fall into. Each time, it's harder to keep my footing. So hard do I work to protect him that there are moments when even I begin to believe that there's hope. I think about miracles. I think that if time is on our side, a full recovery might still be possible. But it doesn't last. Often, when I'm alone, I cry. In the Metro all I have to do is walk past a street musician to fall apart. I feel remote from everything, especially other people. I can't forget that not long from now the day will come when my father won't be here. I feel his defenselessness as my own, and it makes me even sadder to think that his life has been incomplete, that he'll exit it unfulfilled, with business left undone. I know this is a presumption I'll never be able to confirm, but that's what makes me saddest. Not so much the loss of him as the possibility that he'll die with the feeling that he's been a failure.

It's likely that my father's inability to understand the negative effect of some of his actions on me arose from the comparison of his own circumstances with mine, in particular his relationship with his father. It's a supposition, but suppositions say something about us too.

First and foremost, I had a mother. First and foremost, I had a father like the father he would have liked to have had.

And on top of that, my childhood and early youth were spent in much freer and more stimulating times than his.

If only I'd been lucky enough to have a life like his, he must have said to himself.

And I, on the other hand, didn't realize how difficult his life might in some respects have been, and when I did realize it, I didn't consider that this excused certain debts he owed me. Debts of responsibility, involvement, reciprocity, and also financial commitment, to the extent that this backed up the others.

When he didn't have money, I never asked him for it or minded that he didn't share expenses with my mother.

But I did ask him for it and I did blame him in a thousand different ways for not helping when he did have it, though often he didn't know he had it.

That was the problem.

That generally he didn't know.

And as a result, his resentment at feeling himself treated unfairly sometimes led him to commit other injustices that lengthened the list of charges.

The main one: believing that my discontent was only material, thus ascribing to me all the petty motives—never explicitly mentioned or even insinuated—that such an accusation presumed.

Though he could see for himself that my discontent lingered even when he was generous with me.

Money was part of it, but more than that, it was everything he should have done for me and didn't do, because he was forbidden to; everything he didn't do and simply didn't know that he should do; everything he did do but did in secret; and everything he didn't do, fearing my reaction.

It's hard for me to cloak our perpetual rift in logic. It isn't that the logic strikes me as prosaic or puerile, or that time and experience have made it meaningless. What sometimes seems prosaic and puerile to me is my determination not to give in. I should have been more conciliatory. The first to forgive.

In the end, I always knew that either he wasn't aware of his failings or he hadn't weighed the consequences, and that he suffered as much as I did from the effects on me.

But why did I always have to be the generous one? Why was I the one who had to make do and put up with everything?

And how could he permit himself not to see, not to notice, not to weigh the consequences?

I know that when my financial situation was at its most desperate, it tormented him. I know he suffered. Without being asked, two friends of his recently said as much, and both were very explicit.

But why didn't he open his eyes, then?

Occasionally I did say to him that his finances didn't add up; occasionally I did say to him that he was deceiving himself about money. And he must have been aware that there was something to what I was saying, because for a long time, whenever he sold a painting, he did everything he could to hide it from me.

Occasionally I did complain that when he gave me something, it was always in secret; occasionally I did complain that we saw each other only for lunch, and almost always on Tuesdays, when it was easiest for him to hide it. And he must have been aware that there was something to what I was saying, because when he was alone in Madrid, he broke with all the imposed routines and did all he could to see me more often than usual.

Such insecurity. Such a way of being. Such fears.

He lived in fear of life's uncertainties; he lived in fear of being left with nowhere to turn; he underestimated his abilities; he thought that on his own he would go under, and he clung to the life raft that the friend he met in Brazil lent him on punishing terms, without realizing that it was his own two legs that were carrying him.

He felt indebted for a life raft cobbled together of scraps that cost him sweat and tears, and he trusted and trusted and trusted in the future, waiting perhaps for me to grow up, waiting perhaps for a stroke of luck that would pay him his due, and pay me mine, too.

And in matters where no one would have thought of hindering him, it's likely that all of the above made him feel so trifling that he didn't think he had the right to intervene.

But he shouldn't have and couldn't make his surrenders mine; he shouldn't have and couldn't make me yield and inherit his capitulations.

He had abdicated his authority, but he shouldn't have and couldn't make me abdicate with him.

And ultimately that was what he wanted.

Today I had lunch plans with an old friend of his, also a painter. We met at his house, he showed me his paintings, and then we went out to lunch at a neighborhood restaurant where we were joined by a friend of mine who spent time with my father toward the end of his life. Everything was so much like what he and I used to do together that he was constantly on my mind, and though in general I try to avoid the subject and not harp on his failings or my grievances, I ended up talking about him. So many times in the past I'd talked to my father about this friend of his that doing the reverse inevitably made me feel uncomfortable.

My friend opened fire by asking whether it was regret or liberation that my father had felt most strongly in the end, when, faced with betrayals like those he had long forgiven, he gathered strength that he didn't have and took the step that for years he hadn't dared to take. My friend thought that he must have felt liberated, but my father's friend and I corrected him. It's hard to see it any other way. If liberation was what he felt, why choose the worst possible moment to act? If liberation was what he felt, why the wait? He must have felt regret. It was the support he had from so many of us that allowed him to act, and it's likely that then he felt something like relief, but how to erase the previous twenty years, how to erase the things that had happened, how to erase the hostility created between us? No. He must have felt terrible regret. Though his final act of rebellion guaranteed that at least not all was regret, he must have felt cheated.

Or not.

Maybe it was another way of making amends to ensure his recovery. One of the temptations of those who've suffered some trauma is to think that it's a punishment and that everything will be all right once the wrong is righted.

A guilty conscience. Magical thinking.

Or maybe, presented by death with the chance for a grand gesture, he did it just to erase the enmity between us.

But I'm getting ahead of myself. I'm making the same mistake that I may have made with him: living in anticipation, thinking I know what he'll do.

I'll talk later about survival strategies—his and mine—in the face of illness.

The point is that after this sterile debate with my friend and my father's friend, I went on to tell them about the unnecessary cruelties he suffered during his illness, and once I'd begun, I came up with some examples that give a good sense of the magnitude of the self-deception in which he'd lived up until that point, and of my belief—which might seem exaggerated but in fact isn't so exaggerated—that for some time, while imagining himself to be sheltered and protected, he was really the one providing shelter and protection. I explained all this even though it wasn't new to them, and then my father's friend said something he had mentioned on another occasion, to which I hadn't wanted to pay too much attention: he said that my father wasn't happy, that for the last ten years he'd been subdued, not his usual self, trapped in an unfulfilling partnership. Though my father's friend didn't include me as a cause of this unhappiness, while he was speaking, I thought that if what he said was true, I had contributed to it; that if I had stood unconditionally by his side, if I hadn't complained, if I hadn't constantly been throwing his behavior in his face, he would have been less unhappy. And if it's possible to repent of something while knowing that if you had another chance, you'd make the same mistake, I've repented.

I would do it all again. Why lie?

Though this is a labor of love, it must be said, I don't always know how to liberate myself from memory.

I have to ask where all this weight comes from.

Everything—the good and the bad—was intensified because our relationship was exclusive, because I was an only child. But it's also possible that this was precisely what saved us. If he couldn't support one child, if he couldn't give that child all that was demanded of him, how could he possibly have succeeded with two or three?

And maybe everything would have fallen apart more drastically.

Or maybe not. Maybe his commitment and sense of responsibility would have been greater.

I don't know. Who knows?

Though my job is supposedly that of imagining lives, I can't imagine the different possibilities of my own.

What's certain is that my father's presumed unhappiness—if the dissatisfaction I frequently noted in him deserves the name—wouldn't have ended if he'd had me unconditionally by his side. He would have had fewer things to worry about, that's all.

And by the same token, nor am I sure that the source of this presumed unhappiness was the lack of understanding between him and the friend he met in Brazil.

Outside the bedroom, they had nothing to say to each other. Moments of tension seemed more frequent than the moments of peace when they shared silly jokes. They had no common interests. They argued constantly. My father couldn't count on her in matters crucial to him, and meanwhile, she was in pursuit of a goal—his complete surrender to her—that she never quite managed to achieve, among other things because it required my complete annihilation.

That's what I observed and what my father's friends now tell me was going on.

But they were together for more than twenty years.

Clearly there was something there beyond my father's need for protection.

Not just sex, which was probably the original cement of their union.

He accused her of jealousy, of being obsessed with money, and sometimes, I'm told, he was embarrassed by her, but of course he loved her.

It would wane over time, it was subject to ups and downs, and the logic that sustained it wasn't always the same, but there was love. A love not of equals, a love that in my father's case involved a strange moral superiority that led him to forgive her whims, her impositions, her larcenies, seeing them as weaknesses of character—but love.

And it's likely that the reason he let her get away with so much, the reason he yielded to her, the reason he sometimes seemed like a broken doll in her hands, lies in that strange moral superiority.

And it's likely that here, too, lies the reason for their unresolved conflicts, the reason she felt threatened, the reason for her war with everything in his life that didn't include her.

None of these possibilities can be ruled out. What's more, I'm convinced that they're true.

Similarly, it's likely that my father never stopped to consider the consequences that his capitulations would have for me, since—the affection we felt for each other being unquestionable, despite our problems—he demanded from me a moral superiority equal to his own. Blood of his blood, I should hoe the same row.

That was it.

And meanwhile, in January 2006, complications arise that postpone his release. Anxious about the delay to the start of his treatment, I convince them to let him go, but the next day he's admitted again with a high fever. New tests, pleas to the doctors, attempts to grease the rusty wheel of the hospital. The friend he met in Brazil makes herself scarce. It's he and I who push.

His eyes show clear relief each time I arrive at the hospital. Still, I'm not always there, and I can't control what happens when I'm gone: the pressures, the meddling, the ill-timed demands of the friend he met in Brazil. All I hear are the bits and pieces that he passes on to me. She tells him, it seems, that his illness will be very expensive, that he'll need home care and she won't be able to pay for it. She asks him for money, and one day she transfers to her own account an important sum that he's just received for the sale of some prints. My father tells me all this without hiding how upset he is. He's hurt that she seems less concerned about his well-being than about looking out for herself. He's stunned. He never considered her capable of such a thing. He knows she doesn't need the money; years of obsessive saving have left her well covered. Because of this, and because the assumption that she's preparing for a life without him is to accept something that neither he nor I is yet willing to contemplate, he finds it hard to believe.

It's nerves, he tells me sometimes. She's like a child, and it's all too much for her. "When I get out of the hospital, she'll calm down," he adds, to take the sting out of it. At other moments, however, he begins to talk about separating from her. He's like a kid fantasizing. He won't tell her until he's out of the hospital and back on his feet. He's wary of her tricks, the snares she might set for him.

He talks to me in bursts. He tells me things he's never told me. He criticizes her, ridicules her, accuses her of being greedy, says that she has the brain of a mosquito, and suddenly the next day he's defending her again. These are brief moments. Flashes. Most of the time he keeps quiet. Most of the time he doesn't want to think. Tense, preoccupied, he clings to any distraction. Maybe by denying it, by refusing to acknowledge it, it will go away. Essentially it's the same kind of behavior that's always governed him. But not wanting to think about something is already a way of thinking about it. He avoids asking himself why she acts the way she does, but secretly the question is asked and answered.

Consequently, each day he and I grow closer. *I* entertain him; *I* deny what he wants to deny. We watch television, talk about things of no consequence, take walks down the hallways, poke fun at other patients, make plans for the future, break the rules in small ways, like eating takeout from KFC when the nurses aren't watching.

One afternoon I confess that I'm feeling the urge to become a father, and he advises me against it, telling me how exhausting it is to have a child, and then he realizes the incongruity of what he's said and tries to make up for it by complimenting me. I don't know what's more pleasing to me: the rather obligatory declaration of love with which he corrects himself or the masculine camaraderie that for a few instants seems to make him forget that we're related.

And there's his tact—inflected with modesty, which always surprises me—in his dealings with others. The nurses, the doctors, his roommates . . . With everyone he displays an almost pathological humility. With some of the nurses, too, he flirts timidly, a bit perplexed, sometimes, by their excessive familiarity. He's bothered by the brusqueness, the lack of formality, their casual way of speaking to him and their habit of treating him with the condescension of people used to dealing with patients, their habit of talking to him as if he were a child or an old man. His favorites are the ones who don't talk to him that way. When his departure approaches, he asks me to buy them presents. It must be hard for a man in his condition, who was once attractive and who always liked women so much, to expose himself to the female gaze. It moves me to realize this for the first time. The speed with which he hides his belly when one of the nurses comes in, his outsize efforts to spare them any contact with his body.

It moves me.

The last days are the worst. The friend he met in Brazil still hasn't taken responsibility. She misses whole days at the hospital, and when she appears, she stays for only a little while. One morning she says that since he won't be able to work, they'll have to sell the house they own together and use his share of the proceeds to defray the cost of his illness. Another time she talks to him about mortgaging his part of the house. Afraid that this is simply a ploy to leave him with nothing, my father refuses the mortgage but accepts the sale, with the intention of separating, he tells me, as soon as it's accomplished.

"If she's so worried, why doesn't she sell one of her other houses instead of making me leave my house and studio, sick as I am?" he asks me.

I'm silent. I could come up with excuses for her, reassure him, but I don't.

Meanwhile, the fever hasn't subsided, but I manage to convince the doctors that it may not be caused by an infection, as they fear, but by the tumor, and after several anxiety-ridden days in which he leaves everything in my hands, I persuade them to let us go.

The release has an immediate beneficial effect. It's only logical. In addition to leaving behind the weariness and despair brought on by such a long stay, exiting the hospital means beginning the treatment, and beginning the treatment means beginning to recover. At least as he understands it.

On his first day of freedom, I take him home. He's tired, but in good spirits. The friend he met in Brazil greets him with a show of cosseting to which he responds curtly. At one point, when she goes out of the room and leaves us alone, he raises his fists to his temples, pricks up his index fingers, and calls her Beelzebub. I laugh.

For the next few days, until the beginning of the treatment is set, I ferry papers back and forth from the hospital. They explain the routine to me and I explain it to him. It'll be every other Wednesday. He'll have to show up at eight in the morning for tests and return at eleven to be hooked up for five hours. Then, until Friday afternoon, he'll wear a plastic bottle that will continue to introduce a gas into his bloodstream. That's when I tell him what I've had the hardest time coming to terms with: first they'll have to implant a catheter near his shoulder, in something the doctors call a reservoir, an access port to the body. I've been in the chemotherapy room, and I know it isn't something that all the patients have, but I don't mention this, not wanting him to ask me for the explanation that I was given. No one has told me whether it'll ever be removed, whether it's planned that one day he'll stop being a cyborg. No one seems to contemplate the possibility. But he doesn't seem concerned. All he cares about is starting to get better. The day of the procedure, he's happy when he comes out, declaring how simple it was.

The following Wednesday we arrive at the scheduled time. The patients go in for the testing in fives. Some—most—have come alone. Some hide the patchy balding of their skulls under wigs or scarves. Some speak among themselves as if they've known one another for a long time. They have encouraging words for each other and they remark upon how well one or another supposedly looks, while my father takes refuge in his shyness with a patrician air that his excessive humility fails to hide. I joke with him, trying to turn his gaze from the most ravaged, until his turn comes. Then we go out for breakfast. We're both afraid of the side effects. We don't know whether he'll lose his appetite or his hair; we don't know whether he'll vomit or grow weak. It's a time of unknowns, but also of apprenticeship. Back at the hospital, the nurses address him by name when they speak to him, just as they do the other patients who doze connected to sophisticated blue drips, and he smiles, amazed by their powers of retention, grateful for the deference, though he's aware, I suppose, that it isn't by chance, that it's on the instructions of the psychologists. Over the next few hours his sister comes, a friend comes, and finally, the friend he met in Brazil comes . . . In the afternoon, we're alone again. It worries my father that I haven't gone back to see my wife since his operation, and we agree that from now on, I'll split my time: one week with her and one week in Madrid, coinciding with the treatment days. At first he refuses even this, but then he accepts. He doesn't say so, but it's plain that he needs me. It's plain that he's grateful and moved. Maybe that's why he tells me that the friend he met in Brazil has replaced the lock on the door to their house and hasn't given him the key, so he can't make me a copy. She claims that while he was in the hospital, I came to the house and stole the holographic document, drawn up years ago, that lists their respective belongings. Of course I'm indignant at this false accusation, and if my father harbored any doubts, he dismisses them when he sees my reaction. My anger is so great at being repaid like this for what I'm doing that when it's time for us to leave that afternoon and they attach the bottle he'll have to wear until Friday, I take him home but don't come inside with him, out of fear that I won't be able to control myself if the friend he met in Brazil is there.

The next morning, we head to the hospital again, where

he has his final appointment with the surgeon who operated on him. Then we go walking to meet my mother for lunch. The walk is long, but he feels so good that we speculate jokingly about whether chemotherapy includes some stimulant. Though wintry, it's a bright morning. Before we reach the antique shop where my mother is working while she waits to be able to move to Galicia, we stop for a moment and sit on a bench in front of a nightclub that was famous in the seventies. He asks whether it's still open and I tell him what I've been told: it's now a high-class brothel. We start to talk about sex, and he laments that it's all over for him. Though actually it's not a lament. It's bait for me to contradict him. I do so immediately, and soon he confesses that it's been a while since he slept with the friend he met in Brazil. It's a casual confession, and he makes it clear that he doesn't miss it. I offer to get him Viagra to use with anyone he wants, and he doesn't reject the idea, but suddenly he retreats into a modest silence. Then, casting modesty aside, he reveals bedroom intimacies that confirm the lack of compatibility that I always suspected between him and my mother in that regard. I'm perplexed, I want to know more, but my role is to follow his lead—I talk when he talks; I stop when he stops—and now he's decided to stop.

Five minutes later we get up from the bench. When we reach the antique shop, he goes in first. I'm behind him, so I don't quite hear what he says to my mother; all I see is that he tells her something and then he steps away, overcome by emotion, and raises a hand to his eyes as if to wipe them. Hours later, my mother tells me that he thanked her for the son they share, and it was her reply, thanking him in return, that made his eyes grow damp.

That same day, after lunch, we spend the afternoon with a friend of his. It's the happiest day I've spent with him since he was admitted to the hospital, but not all is bliss. When we get to his house, he's tired and goes to bed. The friend he met in Brazil appears while I'm making him dinner. We haven't seen each other since I learned that she accused me of having stolen from her. I'm the one who brings it up. In a low voice—attempting to be conciliatory, much as it galls me—I try to plead my innocence, but it's hopeless; as soon as I start to speak, she interrupts me, and screaming and railing at me as if I'd tried to assault her, she flees upstairs. When I bring up his dinner, my father, who's heard the racket, asks why I didn't keep what he told me to myself, at which moment she bursts into the bedroom like a hurricane to continue the fight. She accuses me again of theft, she accuses me of coming between them, of conspiring, of plotting to take what belongs to her. I try to make her stop, but I can't. My father tries, but he can't either. Unable to contain myself, I reply sarcastically to the nonsense she's spouting. I ridicule her, I tie her up in dialectical knots. She answers back, getting more and more upset; she raises her hand to hit me, and I hold her gaze with a scornful smile. She doesn't dare land the blow, and it's at this moment that my father, flushed with anger, gives a howl and she abandons the room in tears. Half an hour later I leave the house with a vague feeling of guilt and the well-founded fear that for him the night isn't over yet.

Friday we go back to the hospital for the removal of the plastic bottle that since Wednesday has been insufflating a gas into his system. From now on, the idea is that we'll be able to remove it ourselves, and they offer to show us how. This time the friend he met in Brazil doesn't make herself scarce. She's realized, perhaps, that she's doing herself no favors by failing to show up, and she wants to regain lost ground. But when the nurse who's instructing us suggests that she draw out the needle that attaches the tube to the implant, she exits with an excuse, leaving us alone. That night she tells my father in no uncertain terms that she doesn't want me to be the one responsible from now on. She also warns him that she doesn't want me to spend the night at the house, as at some point she's heard me offer to do.

As my father and I agreed, I go back to my wife the next day. I don't return until a week later, on the eve of his next chemotherapy session. This same sequence will repeat itself for the six months that the treatment lasts: five to seven days in Madrid accompanying him on his trips to the hospital, and seven to nine days in Valencia with my wife. Since I don't drive, all my traveling is by bus, six and a half hours each way, during which I'm not capable of reading or even thinking. When I'm with my wife, I try to work. And yet that whole winter I manage to write only five micro-stories, requested by a painter friend for a portfolio of engravings, and a lecture I'm scheduled to give in April at the Thyssen Museum as part of a series titled The Painting of the Month. I conceived the talk as an explicit homage to my father, and that's why I've chosen to speak about a collage by Kurt Schwitters, in memory of the exhibition we saw twenty-odd years ago at the Juan March Foundation. Meanwhile, I try to get my wife granted a temporary transfer to Madrid for the next school year. I make calls, I fill out forms, I pester everyone who might be able to help us. I periodically inform my father of my efforts and he hardly tries to disguise the relief he would feel to have me permanently nearby, my migratory life at an end. I also go out too much at night when I'm in Madrid. I arrive on Tuesday, stop by to see my father, and slip into the murk, eager to kill time and seized by a deep fatalism that makes it hard for me to answer when someone asks me about him. Often I show up on Wednesday mornings at the hospital without having slept much. My father can tell at a glance. I never deny it, though I trim hours off my escapades. Even then, I don't think I manage to fool him. All he does is meet my eyes, without venturing to give me the recriminatory look with which he used to convey his disapproval. I don't know whether he restrains himself in belated recognition of the fact that I'm a mature adult, which is something that had previously escaped him, given the circumscribed and cautious nature of our interactions, or whether it's his way of compensating for the disruption caused by his illness, as if he considers my antics a necessary diversion from the care I owe him. But I think it's something else entirely. I think his happiness to see me trumps everything, and with his long, searching gaze he's expressing his gratitude that I'm faithfully honoring my commitment to him. The only consolation of a sick man: the fortitude of his successor, his principal legacy, his future life, his own blood.

Everybody tells me so: when I arrive at the hospital, his face changes.

There are places I've never been and places I never want to go. I have to take the bird's-eye view.

This is a story about two people, but I'm the only one telling it. My father wouldn't tell it.

My father kept quiet about almost everything. My father was shy, introverted, and melancholy by nature.

So am I.

One of his multiple birthrights.

We resemble each other.

We resemble each other greatly, but sometimes I have the feeling that I got the worst of him. The gloom, the conformism, the laziness, the inability to get ahead, the fear.

And the best? Our dark sides are similar, but the light comes to us from different places.

My father was shy, introverted, and melancholy by nature, but that doesn't mean he was sad. He hated any kind of solemnity, including the solemnity bred of sadness. His main obsession, it's fair to say, was being happy. He harbored all kinds of doubts about himself and was always grappling with them, but just as zealously he sought distraction, sought to brush his doubts aside. Humor was his tool, the territory in which he moved most easily. He used it to defuse potential conflict, to avoid the gaze of others, to shine in public, to demand affection, to offer affection, to judge the world. Also to defend himself. When he was cornered and forced into a prickly conversation, his initial tactic for dodging blows was a humorous remark. It was his way of asking for forgiveness and obtaining it before running into a dead end. It was his way of buying time when he felt corralled, before a blowup, since his incapacity for dialogue when he was questioned often led to fits of anger.

Since he avoided the spotlight, his jokes weren't stagy; he didn't seek the coda of a laugh. He preferred to wield irony—an irony that could be devastating when he was talking about things that really mattered to him—and, even more frequently when among friends, he resorted to self-mockery, as when he affected the voice of a child to make his demands for love or to respond to those made of him.

I think that what he was hiding was a pronounced, paralyzing sense of pride. Many of his character traits embarrassed him, beginning with sentimentalism, and he put all his energy into hiding them, keeping them safe from prying eyes. That was why he avoided conversations that were too emotionally charged: he feared that his true self would surface, that a tear would escape him or one remark would lead to another until he ended up saying something he didn't want to say. In fact, what embarrassed him most, and what his overdeveloped sense of pride was at most pains to conceal, was that he saw himself as weak. Sentimentalism was something he considered to be part of that weakness, along with other things I can only guess at. The central one: his lack of assurance in facing the practical questions of life, of which I—as his son—was a constant reminder.

For years I accused him of being an egoist, and he was. But it wasn't the egoism of someone who loves only himself, who doesn't care what happens to anyone else; it was the egoism of someone who does care, even too much, but who has a hard time stepping up if his life will be affected.

Did our similarities get in the way of our relationship? I'm not even sure they're real and not a pretense that I clung to in times when nothing else seemed to unite us.

Resemblances: inherited and learned. I've written about them before. In my second novel I loaned my narrator my perplexity about why we're stuck with certain traits—attitudes and mannerisms especially—that seem too random to be genetic and too trivial to be learned.

Most of the odd resemblances I cited as examples in my novel were really my father's and mine. I don't include them here, because they've already been recorded, and when stripped of the mask of fiction, almost all of them embarrass me. I purposely chose them with a parodic slant because that's what the tone of the novel demanded.

Of course, they aren't the only traits we shared. Beyond those I've used in fiction and beyond our increasing physical resemblance, there are others. Learned and inherited. Both of us melancholy, both quick-tempered, both timid, both insecure, both sentimental, both skeptics, both pessimists, both solitary, both allergic to social climbers and posers, both sober, both slightly exhibitionistic, both stoic, both dreamers, both affectionate, both masculine, both heterosexual, both secretly feminine, both vulnerable, both compassionate, both obsessive, both split, both quiet, both hobbled and thrown off-balance by an excessive awareness of our own limitations.

That's part of what I inherited from him. The strange thing is that I could hardly have received it by contagion, having spent so little time living with him. Did it come to me in my genes, or did life mold us similarly even though our circumstances were different? He, a motherless child with older sisters, and I, an only child of separated parents; he, a creature of privilege until suddenly he wasn't, and I, spoiled and pampered until I was made a skeptic by the fragility of the good life my mother and I shared and by the times we plummeted into the void, as well as by my dissatisfaction with him. Maybe that's it: different circumstances with comparable effects. Or it might be that the resemblance isn't so great, as I've said. That it's nothing but an old formula for strengthening the bonds between us, recovered now through the subterfuges of mourning. As if I were trying to eliminate our differences in order to hold on to him, to make the line "Your father lives in you now"—which brought me unexpected consolation and that I could even feel physically—come true.

I don't think that's it. I think we are alike, even though there's no way that all the traits we share could have been handed down to me directly from him; similarly, it wasn't rejection of him that caused me to be inspired by the ways in which we were different, the things that set us apart: he more of a hedonist, more open-minded, more curious, more voracious, more virile; I more malleable, more chameleonic, warier, stronger, more capable, more independent. Less wounded.

It's no accident that I've written "less wounded." For

years I wouldn't admit it; for years, when I had him permanently in the dock, I tried to undermine any justification that might excuse his behavior. If he was wounded, I was more wounded; if his life had been hard, mine was harder; if he had something to complain about, I had more to complain about. He might have been mistreated by life, I thought, but he had mistreated me. Now I realize that this way of thinking itself proved that I'd had an advantage over him. I had him to rebel against, to build myself up against.

Competing with him, thinking that I was better than he was, gave me the impetus that so many times I would otherwise have lacked. Pitting myself against him and drawing strength from my rage, I gathered weapons to survive in the world. Pitting myself against him and drawing strength from my rage, I came up with plots for my stories; pitting myself against him, it's even likely that I became a writer. After all, wasn't the hatching of my dream and the switch to my mother's world a consequence of my prolonged rebellion against having to give up the best playroom I ever had: his painter's studio?

But that's not all I got from him. What I got also includes what I really did learn.

Of what we shared, it's hard to say which things—on his side—were a deliberate search for common ground, and which—on mine—were an attempt to emulate him.

For an endless period—almost my entire adult life—he exasperated me. He exasperated me more than anyone ever has. He exasperated me so much that for long periods I didn't want to see him; just hearing his voice on the phone put me in a bad mood. I was outraged by his resignation, his conformism, the secrets he kept from me. I was outraged by his aloofness, his slipperiness, the way he ignored my arguments. I was outraged by his lack of understanding. I was outraged by his sense of superiority, his social clumsiness, his self-absorption. I was outraged by how fat he was, by the way he dressed, by his increasingly bourgeois life. I was outraged that in order to further refine his irritating stoicism, he had abandoned parts of himself that seemed more attractive to me than what he let me see in that endless stage of our life. It's fair to say that I despised him. So great was my anger at times.

And yet practically all the faults I accused him of were faults of omission. His guilt lay not in what he did, but in what he failed to do, and especially what he failed to do for me. But even there I didn't consider him to be completely guilty. His sin was having surrendered, having succumbed. The true guilty party, I concluded, was the friend he met in Brazil. His suffering was proof of it. If he had been the one driving it all, he wouldn't have felt so bad. But he did. He blamed me, I suppose, for being immature, willful, demanding, but I always believed that when he turned out the lights at night, at the mercy of the radio playing in the background, he forgave me and understood me.

That was the excuse that made it possible for me not to burn the bridges between us.

That was my escape route back to him.

And that's why I could admire him, even though sometimes I despised him.

And I did admire him.

Because it was all a mistake. Because it's likely that if I hadn't needed him so much, if I hadn't missed him so much, if I hadn't been so conscious of my mother's and my vulnerability, I wouldn't have been hurt in the same way by his desertions.

All I wanted was more of him; all I wanted was to spend more time with him.

Because I liked him, because I needed him, because since

I was very little I remember adopting his opinions and making them my own; because if I know how to travel, if I know how to cook, if I know how to hang a painting, if I know how to fix a lamp, if I know how to walk into an antique store or a furniture store and distinguish the authentic from the fake, if I know that the world is round and that nature (nature: I owe that to him too) doesn't make some languages better than others or some countries better than others or some religions better than others, if I know how wrong it is not to rise above one's situation, I owe it in part to him.

All of this though I may have considered myself to be better at everything he taught me, though I may have girded myself in the material hardship of my daily life and intimately despised the comforts for which I believed he had betrayed me.

I inherited his toolbox, and after he left home I had to stand in for him in every instance where domestic equilibrium demanded it, but I never got used to his absence. If I had, who can say whether he would matter to me as much as he does? If I had lived with him every day, I might not have felt such lasting admiration for him.

I wonder, too, whether, in my perpetual anger at him, I didn't blame him for things that weren't his fault; I wonder whether in fact he really was the only one responsible for the rift between us; I wonder whether adversity drove me to make unreasonable demands; I wonder why, considering that I believed myself to be superior to him in nearly every way, I couldn't have taken the crucial step sooner.

But I was weak, I felt alone, and until my life was more or less on track, I couldn't forgive and forget. I had to grow up. I had to accept the way things were, stop thinking about my mother and me, stop worrying about what would happen to us.

The rage I would have saved myself.

And the yearning.

I liked to listen to him talk about painting, go to shows with him; I liked to tag along with him at flea markets, stop in at antique shops or almost any kind of shop, guess what would catch his eye and what he would sneer at; I liked to catch even the slightest remark that he let slip when his guard was down, learn what stimuli he responded to; I liked to watch him with his friends, to delight in the provocative firmness with which he expressed his almost always heterodox views; I liked to listen to music, go to the movies, and drink at the bar with him; I liked to watch television, to walk with him; I liked it when he considered me an equal, an artist, when he let me in on his secrets, when he included me in his plans; I liked to match his dilettantish hedonism, his omnivorous tastes; I liked it when he instructed me, valued my judgment, asked my advice; I liked it when he noticed seeds in me that he had sown, liked to surprise him with my assimilation of his teachings; I liked it that he had in me a listener whose interest increased the less he confided; I liked him to celebrate my successes; I liked to invade his territory, buy something he had bought, go somewhere he would have liked to go, do something he would never have done.

I needed his recognition.

I wanted to learn, to be like him, and I imitated him; of course I did. I tried to emulate him.

But I hardly ever succeeded. I lacked so much of the knowledge that I know he possessed. We squandered so many opportunities. We hardly ever permitted ourselves to be together, and most of those times we were so paralyzed that all we could focus on was outmaneuvering each other. We hardly ever went to restaurants or record stores or out for walks, hardly ever traveled together, hardly ever spent time at the beach (absurd even to mention it).

His fault and mine. His fault for not realizing that this was what I most desired, his fault for doling it out by the dropperful, sheepishly, secretly, in the shadow of his other life, his married life, and my fault for choking the already scanty flow with my perennial anger.

I almost never saw him cook, except for very basic dishes, but the one time he invited me to a dinner at his house he served tzatziki and hummus as an appetizer, and days later I asked for the recipe so that I could make it myself. Another time I discovered a jar of mango chutney in his refrigerator, and soon afterward there was an identical jar in mine.

I didn't have the money to buy a house for myself, but when I played the lottery, the houses that my imagination bought were modeled after his.

When he asked me for the jointed wooden mannequin of the Virgin Mary, a piece he had left at my mother's house, I returned it to him, of course, but it wasn't long before I got one for myself that was as much like his as possible.

We might not talk for weeks, but each morning when I sat down at my desk, I imagined him in his studio, faced with difficulties similar to mine.

And I competed with him.

And I wanted to be better than he was, to show him that I could write and have fun and be a good son and look after my mother without giving up anything, that life didn't scare me.

Too much intensity.

The migratory life. My migratory life will continue until July 2006. Every seven days, on average, I'm back in Madrid. After the difficult month of February, in which we accustom ourselves to the routine of treatment, my father keeping watch over himself and I keeping watch over him, in March everything improves. He tolerates the chemotherapy well, he's strong and optimistic, and as a result, he's able to lead a more or less normal life. When I'm in Madrid, I accompany him to the hospital; we invent nicknames for the people we've come to recognize (Miss Dearly Beloved, a patient who comes with her husband and brother; Miss Dynamo, a nurse who does everything eagerly and enthusiastically); we see shows; we go for walks; we go to the movies (*Brokeback Mountain*, *Crash*) . . . Even his relationship with the friend he met in Brazil, though shaky and punctuated with clashes, seems calmer.

Around this time, on an impulse after a chemotherapy session, he buys himself an ergonomic recliner, which he later nearly returns for being too ugly, but which, with my encouragement, he ends up holding on to throughout his illness. Nestled into it, chewing his fingernails, his feet hooked around the footrest, he'll spend infinite hours each day watching television. Which is all he's able to do later, when his mind and body give out.

But that state of collapse has yet to come. He's still active and alert, and at the end of March his final show goes up. The day of the opening, as always, the friend he met in Brazil makes it her job to take pictures of all those present, and as always, she avoids taking my picture, something that he uses as ammunition in one of their subsequent spats. Though the opening is well attended, sales are modest. Three or four paintings, if I remember correctly, none of them very big. To make matters worse, one of the most important arts sections doesn't publish a review at all, and even after I make the requisite phone calls, the paper I write for gives the show scarcely half a column of type, with a misleading headline, and the painting featured in the accompanying illustration is printed backward. He's greatly disappointed, and so am I. I blame myself for not having insisted more, for not knowing how to get around the editor's lack of enthusiasm. I try to make up for it by bringing people, by seeking out buyers. About one of them, a famous model I know through friends, my father permits himself to boast to the gallery owners without mentioning that the contact is mine. He tells me this himself with a laugh, flaunting his naked vanity. In a way, he acts like a child who's forbidden nothing, as if his pranks and misbehavior were my idea. For the first time, I'm fully the accomplice I never was before.

The apparent dashing of the perhaps excessive hopes he had pinned on the show leaves him deflated. Even so, he still goes up to his studio to paint. He paints to forget, to keep making, to cling to life, to set things right. He paints to escape the worries that never cease.

Around this time, at the beginning of April, I bring him to spend a week in the Valencia town where I live with my wife when I'm not with him. Disoriented, not used to being my guest, he thanks us exaggeratedly for everything: the food, the walks, the movie sessions—the freedom, essentially, we give him to decide what to do at any given moment. At the train station on the way back to Madrid, when he sees a girl with a brightly colored bag of gummy candies, he expresses a passing interest in trying them. It's my wife who, despite his demurrals, goes with him to the store and buys him a similar bag. He wolfs down the contents on the train, and then I buy him a couple of bourbon and Cokes. It's our way of telling him that everything is fine, that he isn't as sick as he thinks he is.

Around this time, I go with him to an opening at a bank. The show is a selection of contemporary Spanish painting. Hanging on the walls are paintings by several generations of artists, not including my father, and among the guests are museum directors and top critics. The cocktail reception comes to a hilarious end when the floor of the tent where it's held begins to sag under the weight of the arriving guests. Safe in a corner, margaritas in hand, bitter but cheerful, we watch the ludicrous scene.

Around this time, I continue my efforts to get my wife a transfer to Madrid for the following school year so that I can put an end to my migratory life, as my father constantly encourages me to do. I compose a blunt official request that makes my wife cry, in which I cite his need for care, and meanwhile I keep calling anyone who might be able to pull strings.

In April, too, toward the end of the month, I give my Thyssen lecture on Kurt Schwitters. My father has already read it, but he's proud and moved when we leave the museum. His friends and mine are there, his sister is there, his cousins are there, my mother is there, my wife is there, my wife's sister is there.

Days later, as April turns into May, he confides that he has two wishes, contradicting the apparent docility with which he's let himself be deceived about his illness: he wants to apostatize, to renounce the Catholic faith into which he was baptized, erase himself from the church's records, and he wants to make a living will requesting that his life not be artificially prolonged and that, if it comes to it, euthanasia be administered. He takes care of the former himself after overcoming a few hurdles, which he tells me about, delighting in the folly of the successive clergymen who try to make him change his mind. For the latter he needs the participation of someone who will represent him when he can no longer make decisions for himself. Neither when he informs me of this—taking for granted that the representative will be me—nor when, days later, we go to a notary to draw up the document, does he show the slightest sign of grief. On the contrary. It isn't just that the decision brings him relief; if it weren't for the seriousness of the matter, one might say that it elates him. He even laughs in glee about an initial failed attempt to draw up the papers with a notary whom we chose at random and from whose office we fled, joking about his Christian last name, when we discovered that he wasn't willing to do what we asked.

Around this time, in May, the uneasy armistice that he seemed to have reached with the friend he met in Brazil begins to splinter. They've put their shared house up for sale on an Internet site, and although he trusts that they'll keep living together, he doesn't yet understand her drive to sell. Regarding his worries about leaving the house and what a headache it will be to find a place for the paintings that he stores in the top-floor studio, he keeps me insistently up to date. Never, however, does he spell out the perverse logic evident behind her maneuvers; I don't know whether he hasn't processed it or whether, suspicious and fearful of ill omens, he prefers to feign ignorance. Either way, it's surprising but not inexplicable that she insists on selling; it's surprising but not inexplicable that despite her natural inclination to save, she doesn't want to buy a new house but rather suggests that they rent; it's surprising but not inexplicable that she hasn't foreseen that he'll need a place to continue to paint as long as he's able. The explanation is simple, but I can't point it out to my father, because doing so would be like telling him that he really is going to die. So I keep my mouth shut and wait, insisting only—since it's a way of giving him hope—that he should earmark part of the money that he gets from selling the house for the purchase of a studio where he can keep working. Her response is that it can be rented, too, but my father, whether because mistrust has set in or because he's worried about the fate of his paintings, stands firm. Then begins an endless back-and-forth in which the friend he met in Brazil, offering to help him find a studio, tries to reduce the amount set aside for it by searching for something far from the city center, while I argue for a place nearby that he can actually use. More hard bargaining accompanies the initial attempts to sell the house, which she wants to do without his help, nearly making them the victims of an elaborate scam by some alleged Israeli investors who contact her by email.

And meanwhile, my father has to keep struggling with the phantoms his illness conjures up. His doubts are constant, as are his questions and the traps he sets to catch me out. He seems to want the truth, but he wants it to favor him, and so long as I give him half-truths and offer him help and support, he continues to turn to me, to make me his main support. Doing this doesn't trouble my conscience. I give him what I believe he wants, never asking myself whether I'm doing right. I fool myself, too; I too want to believe that if he keeps fighting, he might still live for a few years. I operate in a permanent daze, with just two goals: to ensure that he suffers as little as possible and to ensure that the friend he met in Brazil doesn't leave him penniless. Though the two objectives occasionally coincide, they aren't identical. Untangling them isn't easy, and I often make mistakes that I soon regret.

I let things come as they may. Possibly I force him to be too vigilant, thus obliging him to contemplate what I'd actually prefer that he not contemplate: what's behind the behavior of the friend he met in Brazil.

Around this time, midway through May, we take a night train to Galicia to see the work being done on my mother's future house, where she'll retire at the end of the year. We have dinner in our compartment in the sleeper car, a picnic prepared by me that concludes with whiskey from a flask. In the morning we spend a few hours in Santiago, and that afternoon, when we come to the town where the house is, I can see his surprise at what my mother and I have been able to do. A whole lifetime of lack of trust in us and subsequent flight—wiped away on the spot. Later I'll learn that the impression was lasting, as for months he proclaimed his admiration for our worker-ant labors to anyone who would listen.

Around this time, a trustworthy notary is found, and he signs the living will that was delayed after our escape from the other notary's office.

Around this time, at the end of May, I have to decide whether to accept the invitation of an Italian foundation to write for two months at a villa in Tuscany. At first I can't bring myself to abandon my father, but with his encouragement I accept a stay for half of the time after convincing a friend of his to take my place at the bimonthly chemotherapy sessions. In the same room where Bruce Chatwin wrote some of his books, I spend the month of June in Tuscany, starting and almost finishing a story that has nothing to do with what I'm living through. Meanwhile, thanks to a friend of my father's, my wife's transfer to Madrid for the upcoming school year seems feasible for the first time, and along with it, the end of my migratory life. Meanwhile, my father calls me frequently. I know that he's still painting almost every morning. I know that he takes a short trip or two with the friend he met in Brazil, and that on one of these trips he drives the car. I know that they find buyers for the house at last. I know that he demands that the money due to them be paid in two separate checks, and that because of this and other things, relations between them grow more acrimonious.

I return from Italy on July 5, full of uncertainty about the immediate future. In view of the fact that my father plans to spend August with the friend he met in Brazil at her house in the south, I hesitate between a similar solution that will allow me to continue to accompany him on visits to the hospital, or a trip with my wife—intended as compensation for my constant absences—to Kenya, where my father's older sister has been living for years. But based on a routine scan, which shows that the tumor is active again, the doctors halt his treatment with plans to start a new one in September; and in the office that same day, to mitigate the effect of the news, I ask my father whether he's capable of traveling to Kenya. The answer is yes, and it's immediately clear how excited he is by this unexpected prospect. The friend he met in Brazil chooses not to come, but he decides that he will. Meanwhile, the buyers of the house reach a decision too, and on July 10 the contract is signed and my father receives his part of the down payment. The next day, he asks me to go with him to the bank to deposit it, and he makes me a cosigner on his account.

The trip to Kenya is planned for the end of the month, and on the fifteenth, my father goes with the friend he met in Brazil to her beach house. He returns to Madrid on the eve of our trip. More than tired, he's heavyhearted. He doesn't say so, but it's clear that a line has been crossed. With him he's brought a marquetry box holding four old bullfighter figurines, the only thing he managed to grab reflexively when, minutes before he got into a taxi to the train station, the friend he met in Brazil, like someone granting a onetime chance, offered to let him take whatever he wanted from a house that he thought of as his, too, a house that was absolutely crammed with paintings, furniture, and objects he'd amassed over the years.

In Kenya, things go from bad to worse.

In Kenya we have one good week, during which he's giddy, up for everything; we visit Nairobi and Mombasa and go on a short safari, but our luck changes after a hellish bus ride that can be blamed solely on my desire to present him with interesting experiences. When we reach the island where my aunt lives, he's running a fever; he's done in. When he doesn't feel better with rest, we fear that it's a resurgence of the illness or that—the height of bad luck—he's caught malaria. We're so terrified by the former possibility that we come to hope that it's the latter, and it's hard for us to hide our disappointment when he's tested at a dispensary and the test comes back negative. Obliged to fear the worst, we visit a bare-bones private clinic where the one and only doctor, wearing a Barça T-shirt, attends with admirable courtesy to our first-world concerns. He takes my father's blood pressure, instructs a veiled Muslim nurse to draw blood, and examines it under a microscope. This is all he can do for us, and like all doctors when they don't know what to do and the only thing that matters is that they seem to be doing something, he does it in full awareness of its futility. Later, I get in touch through my mother with my father's oncologist, and though he calms us by saying that he doesn't think it's tumor fever but instead a kidney inflammation brought on by the jolting of the bus, I secretly begin to think about repatriation. Meanwhile, he tries his best to put on a show of strength. He takes walks around the medina, comes to the beach, and even attempts once or twice to go for a sail, but every evening the fever makes its punctual appearance. Each morning we think that it won't come, and it almost always does. And yet, so hard does he try not to let us down, or so badly does he want to recover that he manages to fool me, and sometimes I grow impatient when he limps behind or shows little interest in the plans I'm constantly devising for him. Still, there are good days. Still, he laughs often and freely.

Still, he's in on all kinds of mischief. The main thing he frets over: buying gifts for his nurses and doctors at the hospital.

If this were fiction, I should already be lowering the sails.

Have I gotten to where I wanted to go?

The reasons that make you start writing a book aren't necessarily the same ones that make you keep going when you're halfway through, or the ones that make you end it. In the end, you just want to get to the end.

That's where I am.

I just want to get to the end. The end of the book. The end of my father. The end of my life with him.

To know where we got stuck—that's what I said I wanted at the beginning.

A rhetorical device.

We got stuck in lots of ways. We got stuck where everyone gets stuck. We got stuck because we thought that life was infinite, which is an error in calculation that prompts the worst missteps. We got stuck because he didn't have the stamina to hold on to me and I didn't have the courage to let go. We got stuck because he was brought up to keep quiet, to avoid calling things by their names, and I was raised in the world of my mother, which was a world of words. We got stuck because we weren't the same, or very different either. We got stuck because he had shrunk the perimeter of his defenses to a handspan and I still believed in fighting battles on open ground. We got stuck because his consummate solipsism made him accept the unspoken and I demanded action. We got stuck because we both thought we deserved more than we had. We got stuck because he didn't know how to grow up and I didn't either. We got stuck because we shared my mother, someone he might have preferred to be a distant memory if I hadn't existed, but who for me was a daily reality that I felt obliged to defend and vindicate beyond the necessary. We got stuck because, as a result of this, we had different views of the past. We got stuck because I made him the creditor of a debt that I tried to call in when it had already expired. We got stuck because life's greatest lessons often come too late.

Such a lot of life. Of stuck life.

What did we learn in the final stretch?

That we wasted time. And that things always have an end, and when that end comes, it's better if it finds us at peace.

What everyone always and forever knows.

And what we knew as well as anyone.

Is this what we spent our final year doing? Making sure that when the end came, we would be at peace with each other?

Was it all a fiction? A charade?

What would our future lives have been like if the boundary imposed by his death had suddenly been erased? A new and miraculous cure; his sudden recovery.

I wouldn't have had the strength to go on. He wouldn't have had the stamina to go on.

We would have gone back to being what we were.

Less at odds, more conciliatory, but unchanged.

There was no room for anything else.

Was there space for him in my life? Would he have been capable of making a separate life for himself?

I think it was a conscious choice, being the way he was with me in the end; he knew what he was doing and why.

Because he was going to die.

I've often wondered how well I succeeded in my efforts to keep him in the dark.

But I know I failed.

I think he was asking to be deceived and that he deceived himself; it's likely that when he got sick, he bet on the youngest and most dependable horse, the one that could be relied on for what was to come, but I think that he didn't deceive himself fully, and deep down he knew.

And because he knew, he did what he did.

He wanted to close the circle as best he could.

Even in the face of doubt.

And the circle is closed.

Who worked hardest for it?

He did.

Who was in the biggest hurry?

He was.

Who risked more?

He did.

It wasn't easy. Easy would have been what he didn't do.

My devotion had a day after. His didn't.

And there was a reward for me, though it was only what tradition or common sense dictates.

I'd have done the same if I'd known that I wouldn't get it (as it was, for a long time I didn't know that I would). Though it's likely that in that case the circle wouldn't have closed. Not for me and not for him.

And what about her, the friend my father met in Brazil? This is a book about two people, as I've said, and it's not my aim to unearth her motives. Why did she act the way she did? Was it greed, immaturity, egoism? Whatever the determining factor, it doesn't matter. Maybe greed was the childish tool of her egoism that she wielded to enable her to step out of the picture, to reject a responsibility she was incapable of assuming. That's the best-case scenario. Or worst case, maybe the failure of her egoistic aspirations was the immature fruit of her excessive greed.

I can judge her, but it isn't my mission to redeem her or condemn her.

More essential, anyway, is to determine the mark that her actions left on my father.

And the mark changed over time.

It began as incredulity, turned into silent disenchantment, and ended up as contemptuous indifference.

Did he really not see it coming?

When the signs were already alarming, he continued to make excuses for her.

He made excuses for her in order to retroactively excuse himself.

Or he made excuses for her because he wasn't yet convinced that he was going to die, and knowing that I would be with him on every front of his illness, but not every front of his life, he still needed a life after his illness.

Or he made excuses for her because he still believed her to be innocent. A schemer, with the brain of a mosquito, as he said, but innocent.

That's the answer, I think.

I guess.

Thus the confusion, the silent disenchantment, the contemptuous indifference. The great rancor with which he repaid her toward the end. His stubborn refusal to engage in dialogue with her. His ill will.

There was no going back once he thought he saw her as she was. All his efforts were directed at keeping away from her.

When he confronted his illness, when he contemplated the possibility of his death, it made him want to do right by me. And in the best of worlds, doing right by me shouldn't have meant ruining things with her.

But we don't live in the best of worlds.

And he saw her true face, and when he saw it, he pushed her away forever.

And in a way it was as if he was relieved of a tension that had been building for a long time. As if the decision brought him new strength.

But by that point there was no hope.

And he knew it. By then he finally knew it.

This brings me to a paradox: my father gave himself to me fully only when he knew that there was no hope, and to the extent that it was she who opened his eyes, I should be grateful to her. In fact, it could be said that she did me a favor without realizing it.

But at what cost?

It's a question I'm afraid to answer.

At the cost of obliging my father to face his fate, of stripping the veil from his eyes, of ensuring that if any possibility remained of keeping him deceived, that possibility was destroyed.

Her behavior made it impossible for him to hope, and for a person so fragile, so fearful of almost everything, especially of death itself, this meant consigning him irrevocably to his fate.

No matter what I did, no matter the time I spent reworking each piece of bad news—aided by my skill with words and his faulty memory—to make it seem neutral or even positive, the negative attitude of the friend he met in Brazil, who was so plainly gunning for the day after, was much more persuasive. I managed to deceive him for a long time, or rather for some stretches of that time, but there came a point when it was impossible to keep it up.

The day my father gave the final *no* to the friend he met in Brazil was the day he gave a *no* to himself.

Would his prospects have improved if he hadn't had to give himself that *no*? Would he have lived longer? Would he have beaten the odds, those odds that always leave room for doubt, or so the doctors claim once they've delivered their miserable diagnosis and worse prognosis and—maybe with the intention of preventing the collapse of the patient and his caretakers—they allow themselves to extend the faintest possibility of hope?

It's clear that she robbed him of that remote possibility, or at least she made it permissible for us to think she had.

But the previous paradox is cruel here.

If I hadn't become a threat, if I had wiped myself from the map, maybe she wouldn't have revealed so plainly the future for which she was preparing, and my father could have continued to have faith.

If I ask myself to what extent her abandonment of him, her preoccupation with the day after, led to the collapse of all hope, I also have to ask myself what might have happened if I hadn't been so present. It's just one link up the chain of cause and effect.

And I do ask myself.

I asked myself while it was all happening, before my father died; I continued to ask myself as I began this book; and though the question is now scarcely brighter than a distant lighthouse glimpsed in memory's eye, I still ask myself.

The intensity has lessened.

The certainty of his death, even when it hadn't come yet, established a reality so weighty and irrevocable, so different from any other reality I'd known, that speculating about what might have been became an arduous, unpleasant exercise.

That's the thing about death, that it's irrevocable. And no

matter how closely we're touched by it, so long as it doesn't take us, life asserts itself in the end.

The dead leave sadness and not a few questions behind them. They oblige us to contemplate our own death and, at the same time, the futility of life, but our understanding fails us in the face of the inarguable reality that everything comes to an end, that there's no redemption, that what wasn't done can no longer be done. After a death that touches us closely, the days go by without improvement. Our bewilderment is as great as it was the first day. The only progress is forgetting and the persistence of life sneaking in through unexpected cracks.

A little while ago, in David Rieff's *Swimming in a Sea of Death*, one of the books I've continued to read about mourning and parents, I noted that among family members of cancer patients it's common to feel remorse for not having done enough. I was also told by a writer friend that sixty-five percent of the terminally ill are abandoned by their partners. The figure seems too high, but even if it were correct, my astonishment at what the friend my father met in Brazil did wouldn't lessen, just as we don't feel less remorse simply because many others also feel it.

Rieff says that no one does everything that could be done, because it would mean giving up one's own life. I did give up mine. I did do everything, and I probably did it not just for the sake of compassion or love, but to right old wrongs.

They're the ones that linger.

I regret, as I've said, not having ended the tension between us sooner. I regret having made him suffer. I regret the lost time. I regret what was left unspoken. I regret having needed him to prove by deeds that he was my father and I his son. I regret having thought about his death. I regret having placed a symbolic value on material goods.

Compared to this, any mistakes I may have made when he was sick pale in the light of my extreme devotion.

I don't regret having left him alone, because I never did.

I don't regret never telling him the truth about his illness. I believed that if he kept hoping, some chance still existed that he would be cured.

But it wasn't to be.

Despite my efforts, he found out in the end, and hope vanished and any notion of beating the odds was an illusion.

There was no room anymore for magical thinking, and still we refused to relinquish our respective roles, his of clinging to life and mine of persuading him that anything was possible.

Why did we do it when there was no longer any hope?

To close the circle, I suppose.

Because to accept defeat by mutual accord, knowing that the end was so foreseeably near, would have diminished the magnitude of our mutual devotion.

He didn't hold back. His sense of guilt probably led him to believe that if he did right by me, he would be rewarded, but when it became clear that not even then would there be hope, he continued to give me his utmost.

In this unvarnished account, there are things I can't ignore, much as I might like: the friend he met in Brazil. It would have been best for all of us if she had passed the test, but she didn't. That I refer to her in such a roundabout way is merely confirmation of the fact.

September comes. The final September.

In September we finally manage to secure my wife a place at a school in Madrid for the start of the year. My migratory life ends, and my multifaceted life begins. In September, after our return from Kenya, my father continues to run a fever and has various intestinal complaints. In September, as in January, the doctors delay the beginning of the new treatment until he feels better. In September, afraid that it might be tumor fever, I'm once again treading the halls of the hospital that I know so well. In September, though my nudging is successful and they start the chemotherapy again, he doesn't tolerate it as well as he did before. In September he no longer feels euphoria, but rather a new weariness often accompanied by nausea and fever. The good days that follow the bad aren't very good at all. He gets tired, doesn't go up to his studio. In September, as we're returning from the hospital one afternoon, he breaks down for the first time and, amid tears of despair, tells me things I once used to fantasize about hearing, though said now and said for the reason that they're said, they break my heart. In September the sale of the house is confirmed. The closing will be in December, at the buyers' request. In September the friend he met in Brazil rejects my final attempt to keep my father from having to take such a psychologically difficult step and warns him that if he wants her to take care of him, he'll have to put his share of the money from the sale at her disposal. In September my father says no. In September, taken aback, incredulous, the friend my father met in Brazil asks me in his presence whom he'll live with when they give up the house, and with barely contained rage, my father breaks in to say that it won't be with her. In September, then, we draw up plans for our future together: he'll live with my wife and me in the apartment that my mother will turn over to us when she leaves for Galicia in October, which means that work will need to be done, since the apartment has only one bathroom and my father wants one for his own use. In September the friend he met in Brazil begins to spirit away fixtures and objects, taking the most valuable furniture, too, and in response, each time I come to visit, my father entrusts me with some of his belongings for safekeeping. In September, after being woken one night by a loud noise and discovering that it's her rummaging in his studio, my father entrusts me with the task of finding a place to keep his paintings. We take the most recent ones and his painting tools to a friend's studio and we hire a storage company for the bulk of his work. The day before they pick it up, I help him go through his files, and he dumps most of his papers—personal letters, diaries, photographs—into two big plastic bags that little by little, dividing the contents into smaller bags, he takes out to the trash himself before I can go through with my plans to purge them. In September the keys to his car disappear. In September, upon returning from a chemotherapy session, he finds the house completely empty. The friend he met in Brazil has gone, leaving behind two mattresses, a dilapidated sofa, his ergonomic chair, and little else. In September my father doesn't fall apart. Instead, when his sister, alarmed, comes to visit, he puts on an old Charles Trenet album and for a brief moment, smiling, takes a few turns to the music with one arm folded on his chest and the other outstretched as if he's leading an invisible dance partner. In September he doesn't want to leave the house until the sale is concluded, so my wife and I move in with him. In September the friend he met in Brazil frequently appears unannounced, lets herself in with her own key, and inquires about his health or proposes some plan as if nothing had happened. In September, knowing how painful these irruptions are for him, I suggest that he change the lock, but he refuses, saying that it will only cause more trouble. In September he gives the go-ahead for the purchase of a studio. In September we draw up plans for the renovation of my mother's apartment, where we intend to live, and I start to look for an apartment to rent while the work is being done. In September, while my mother is going through her things in anticipation of her impending move, I embark on an initial cull of my own. I get rid of books, albums, pictures, letters. Practically everything seems superfluous in the certain knowledge that before long I'll have to let go of something infinitely more important. I'm ruthless, the opposite of what I used to be. The more tied I feel to something, the more pleasure it gives me to be able to get rid of it.

At the end of September I'm awarded a residency in Brittany, and again, my father insists that I accept at least a month out of the three I've been offered. I need it. The neglect of my writing weighs on me, I've reached my limit, and a break will help me be better prepared for what's to come. My wife will continue to live with him, and my mother, putting off her departure for Galicia, will relieve her when necessary. Before I leave, he asks me to instruct them not to smother him by trying to make conversation. In my absence, which lasts for almost the entire month of October, he takes walks some mornings, goes out for drinks one Tuesday with his painter friends, attends the opening of a Sargent and Sorolla show at the Thyssen and a Picasso exhibition at the Prado. Most of the time, though, he's at home, watching television from his ergonomic chair. He has closed down his studio, but even if he hadn't, he wouldn't have the strength to paint. His diaries speak of sleepless nights. Encouraged by a friend, he accepts psychiatric help. Meanwhile, in an apartment in the port city of Saint-Nazaire, I try to write a story based on the life I've been living for nearly a year, but I can't get past the first few pages. It feels like the worst kind of betrayal to employ the feelings inspired by his certain death in the service of fiction.

In November, a whirl of activity awaits me upon my return. I travel with my mother to Galicia to help her get settled, and when I get back, I finish clearing out what she hasn't taken with her. I haul junk and household items to Dumpsters; I sort through, tear up, and throw away papers; I sell books for cheap; I bring suitcases of clothes to a church; and I rid myself of keepsakes, at the same time piling up everything to which I still attach some value and covering the piles with plastic tarps. Next, I resume the search for an apartment where we can live temporarily once the sale of my father's house goes through. One morning we return to the notary to have him sign a document giving me power of attorney for my father. He doesn't want to see the friend he met in Brazil again, and he thinks that having me sign the papers as his representative will deal a blow to her pride. Once again I'm his constant companion, his helper in all things, and though sometimes he asks too much of me, he's so grateful that he bridles if he thinks someone else is taking advantage of me or treating me unfairly. Whenever I have a difference of opinion with my mother or my wife, he immediately and uncritically takes my side. But there's also time for entertainment, which I'm always urging on him without doing a very good job of gauging his strength: we frequently go out for lunch; one night we go to see the movie *Capote*, and days later, *The Departed*, with my wife; we visit the studios of a couple of painter friends who want to show him their latest work; we go to the Rastro one Sunday; and one evening, when an actress friend invites us to the theater, we find time for a visit to a nearby cultural center where there's an exhibition of contemporary African painting. Sometimes we talk about the work being done on my mother's apartment, where it's presumed that we'll live, going over the details. More and more often he asks me whether he'll see it finished. At first this seems simply a ploy to furtively probe me about his condition, but in time it becomes an urgent plea, almost a litany. Like the way he tacks the adjective *poor* onto my name to let others know how appreciative he is of my tireless efforts. Most urgent, however, is the search for an apartment where we can live after the sale of the house. It isn't an easy task, since we'll need it for scarcely three months and conventional rentals can't be had for less than a year. I know that he'll consider an apartment hotel an extravagance, and indulging in it will alert him that this is an emergency situation, robbing him of a little more hope. At last, a friend of my wife's rescues us from our fix by renting us two studios, one above the other, near the Plaza Mayor. In the one that can be reached by elevator, we'll set up my father's bedroom and the common areas, and my wife and I will sleep upstairs in the other. I feel as if I've passed a test, just as—ever since he's been sick—I've felt when I overcome some obstacle. To consolidate my top marks, I buy a baby monitor, and before I confirm the rental with my wife's friend, I check that the signal is strong enough to allow us to hear any sound coming from what will be his bedroom. I also decide that when the sale of his house has gone through, it's best if he goes to Galicia to stay with my mother and doesn't return until it's all over, so that the leave-taking isn't as traumatic and he doesn't have to endure the upheaval of the move.

Sometimes those who are about to die rehearse or perform final acts that aren't so much the epitaph that sums up a life as a way of making amends or settling a score that they believe is still pending.

This was my greatest fear for a long time. In some sense— it's clear to me now—I may have begun writing to exorcise it. I was afraid that much of what my father did once he knew he was sick—first with hope and later with the growing conviction, whether articulated or not, that he was going to die— was part of a performance that had me in a privileged seat in the audience. I worried that not all his decisions had been arrived at naturally, as the expression of his desires, and that instead they were shaped by how he wanted to appear before others, especially me. It worried me that, as suggested by events previously discussed, he spent much of his time calculating how to rewrite a part of his life—in other words, that the urge to shape the coming months was fed by the need to correct the past, to strive for a death that would bring to a harmonious close everything in his life that was lacking in harmony; that in all he did, in the decisions he made, there was an element of overacting determined by a past that tormented him. Specifically, the part of his past with which I took issue.

On the other hand, the possibility that there was no overacting or pretense, that he behaved the way he did out of conviction, which would suggest that he really did feel some remorse, was no less frightening. He hinted as much in a thousand ways toward the end. He regretted two things, he said. He didn't rank them: having been inconstant in his career as a painter, allowing himself to be distracted by fleeting romantic conquests; and having neglected his family, for similar reasons.

There's a third possibility, complementary to the latter, which is that his sole intent was to surreptitiously indoctrinate me about my future, as if to say: what I did is what you shouldn't do.

Ultimately, my father faced death the way he had lived: close-lipped, in silence, entirely committed to the idea of himself that he always wanted to project, an idea that wasn't sentimental in the least (though he himself was), that rejected any hint of self-importance, that was allergic to the notion of arousing compassion. Just as, in life, he was terrified of words, terrified of their capacity to reveal his inner self, in his illness, aside from brief laments or the occasional plea for consolation, he didn't allow himself to speak of death. He fell apart only a few times: twice that I know of, and both times when he was alone with me. In public he never complained. Even when what was happening became too calamitous to ignore, he tried to assume an attitude of resignation. His only preparations, shortly after he was operated on—when the progression of the illness hadn't yet made him give up hope of a cure— were to apostatize and make a living will. After those two procedures were completed, he retreated into silence and delegated to me everything that might be necessary from then on: doctors to see, places to live, life itself. He wanted nothing to do with anything. He made just one request of me: that when the moment came, instead of a funeral there would be a party at which his friends could raise a glass.

Once he had accepted death, or at least the possibility of it, the only thing that seemed to trouble him was the image of himself that would linger in the minds of those who knew him. Beyond calling attention to his views on religion by making the symbolic gesture of apostatizing, beyond controlling his own demise to make certain—by means of the living will and my cooperation—that he wouldn't continue to exist past the moment when his mind failed him, beyond orchestrating his own farewell ceremony, his wish was to seem strong in the face of adversity, and in fact he was strong. Strong and brave: I don't think there's anyone who dealt with him who thinks otherwise. Not even the doctors or the nurses. With all of them, even in the worst moments when he was a shadow of his former self, he stood firm. He always had a joke ready to fill the silence left by words that remain unspoken when there's no need to state what's already plain. He sought strength in this, in his need to rise to the idea he wanted to convey of himself, and though the inner self he concealed was much darker and his nights and reflections were doubtless long and desolate, he found what he sought.

He was always observing himself from a distance, always watching himself. He wanted to direct things, guide the plot of his illness and future death, and had it been within his reach, I'm sure he would have kept it up until the end. In addition to the legal proceedings he undertook at the beginning of his ordeal and the instructions he gave for after his death, this is illustrated by two revealing anecdotes.

The first is from the time I took him to see my mother's house in Galicia, when he was still able to lead a more or less normal life, though in a limited way. We were in the train compartment the morning after our departure. We had woken up, he in the lower berth and I in the upper, and after saying good morning, he confessed with a yawn that before he fell asleep he'd thought that he wouldn't mind dying there, safe with his son.

The second is from a few months later, from the trip to Kenya. After our exhausting bus ride, once we had arrived at my aunt's house, I kept watch over him for three nights, his hand in mine, and on the worst night he said, as if to himself, that after all it wouldn't be so bad to die in Africa.

These were the only two times in a year and a half when he referred to his death so explicitly, and both times a kind of manipulative impulse can be glimpsed, as if now that he had gotten used to the idea, what worried him more than death itself was the impression he would make with it. An impression that included the moment and circumstances of its occurrence as well as everything that it brought to a close: his own life, the relationship between us. Ultimately, though different, the two imagined deaths aren't so dissimilar; both feature me as companion and confidant. The first is purely sentimental: the idea of dying with your son while the two of you are happy together; the other is more romantic, with all the exotic associations of a place like Africa. But it isn't only the content that's theatrical here; theatrical too is his reason for making these seemingly inappropriate remarks to me, inappropriate for someone who's near death and who'd be better off not speculating about it. By saying what he said when he did, he was indirectly providing me with an image of himself, helping to define a little better how he wanted me to think of him: as someone strong and with a touch of sarcasm that persisted even in the face of death, and as someone for whom the proper finish meant dying in the company of his son.

Of course, there's nothing wrong with wanting something like that; the end he sought and surely achieved isn't trivialized by his deliberate pursuit of it. As I've said, he drew strength from the image that he wanted to convey, and his behavior wasn't any less genuine as a result.

It's true: sometimes those who are about to die rehearse or perform final acts that aren't so much the epitaph that sums up a life as a way of making amends or settling a score that they believe is still pending.

But don't the dreams into which we project ourselves reveal as much or more about us as our real selves?

You don't lie flagrantly in an epitaph unless you're crazy. You sum up your life, offer your regrets, or project what you once wanted to be.

No one draws strength from emptiness.

Any further speculation would be unjust.

✶

I say goodbye to my father at the airport on November 29, and over the next ten days I visit the notary to sign the contract for the sale of the house, I deposit the check in a joint account, I rent a safe-deposit box for the payment in cash, I pack his clothes; I select—from the scant furnishings that survived the depredations of the friend he met in Brazil—what to bring to the pseudo-duplex that will be our home for the next three months; I perform the move . . . Meanwhile, my father takes walks with my mother, partially recovers his lost appetite, and, most of all, delights in the house in Galicia, which he can't praise enough. I feel as if his approval is my final exam, passed with flying colors. I feel, just as I did when he saw it for the first time, that nothing my mother and I have ever done redeems us so thoroughly, that only our years of relentless saving make us deserving of the trust we were previously denied. I feel that if the house didn't exist, he might not have put himself in my hands as he's done. Later, my mother tells me that the days he spends at the house are an occasion for confidences, too. Apparently, he's more open with her than he's been with me, and he tells her that the only thing that consoles him is the thought that he has something to leave me. Apparently, at some point when my mother was telling him that she still hadn't forgiven her own father for having favored his second wife and her children in his will, my father defended my grandfather's memory, explaining that he probably acted as he did out of weakness and that he himself would have left everything to the friend he met in Brazil if she had taken care of him as she ought. I'm touched by this noble gesture, my father dragging himself through the mud to heal my mother's wound with his own.

But around this time, December by now, I know from his diary that my father is conscious that the end is nearing. His body doesn't respond the way it used to. He's permanently tired. Everything scares him. Everything is a great effort, and the only thing that makes it worthwhile is the affection he feels surrounding him. Just a few weeks ago, difficulties were surmountable because of his will to live. Now, having lost the will, or having come around to the idea that sooner or later his will won't be enough, the only thing that seems to keep him going is his desire not to let others down. Not to let me down, especially. And also, perhaps, his wish to make the most of his time with me, to repay me with this final burst of devotion for everything that we didn't give each other in the past.

He's exhausted when he gets back from Galicia. He won't let anyone meet him at the airport. He takes a taxi to the unfamiliar place where my wife and I are waiting for him and where, though it's only a temporary destination, I've tried to arrange some objects that have always accompanied him: the dresser from his bedroom, a carriage from an electric train he had when he was a boy.

The following days, December days, I lead an exhausting double life. On the one hand, I have to care for him with renewed vigor; on the other, I have to handle matters that could wait but that I need to proceed with to give him the impression that life is going on. I have to supervise the renovation of my mother's old apartment where we're supposedly going to live; I have to start work on the studio where I keep telling him that he'll be able to paint; I have to find a lawyer to set in motion his divorce from the friend he met in Brazil, as he's asked me to do. While I crisscross the city, he scarcely leaves the house, and when he does, I'm almost always at his side. Few are the days when this isn't the case. One afternoon he goes with friends of his, a couple, to a Howard Hodgkin show, and he's so pleased when he gets back that I'm sorry to have missed the chance to once again share the satisfaction he gets from looking at art.

It's rare for him to forget, to come out of himself.

And not because he doesn't try, because he does. He tries to be attentive, he tries to please; he's immediately sorry if his perpetual tenseness (his feet hooked around the extendable footrest of the recliner) makes him snap at someone.

And he makes jokes.

But the day is long and full of hours, and it's hard to turn his waning attention from the television screen. He keeps doing the crossword puzzle from the newspaper, and each day he writes a sentence or two in his diary, but he hardly reads, he can't concentrate. It isn't easy to engage him in conversation, unless it has to do with the progress of the renovation work, about which he's always inquiring. When I'm alone with him, if I ask him about something concrete, he makes an effort not to disappoint me, but he rarely takes the initiative. When he has visitors, his gratitude and happiness gradually fade, and if several people are talking, he eventually falls silent. He has to be asked a question, addressed directly, to be prevented from drawing into himself.

But there are days that are exceptions; moments, especially. In general, his fitful interest in talking is revived by memories that give him the chance to vindicate himself or by subjects so foreign that they manage to distract him. He also has more of a tendency to let loose when the conversation touches—however tangentially—on subjects from which he thinks I can derive some lesson. He complains, as I've said, about not having painted enough, about having wasted time chasing women. To hear him talk, it might seem as if he's weighed down by a sense of guilt and moral failing that he needs to purge, but the truth is that, beyond any tendency toward exhibitionism and vanity, the invocation of his sexual appetite and his need for women actually seems to be the most immediately accessible way to warn me about dissipation, about all those dead-end temptations whose constant pursuit may be, at the end of the day, an excuse for neglecting anything more arduous, time-consuming, or uncertain. Love itself, work, the construction of a living fortress that, by protecting us from the unexpected, allows us to pursue our calling in peace. He doesn't say as much, but what he's warning me against is the sloth of discouragement. What he laments is having shown himself to be vulnerable to setbacks, having allowed himself to be seduced by flight when his work required perseverance.

A couple of times, though in words distorted by an emotion whose source I no longer recall, he goes so far as to say something to me that until only recently was completely unthinkable: *I should have stayed with my family*. Both times I realize that the ambiguity of the noun makes it impossible to say whether he's including my mother or gently excluding her, and I—familiar with mounting waves of feeling dominated by the irrational, and even having come to empathize with the reasons that may have led him to distance himself (ranging from the egoism of someone who would rather seek refuge by himself than risk a shared exposure to the elements, to the tortuous logic of the person who, believing himself to be a burden, prefers not to get in the way of those who will advance faster without him), which I understand not just in an intellectual or abstract way, but through my own experience of the anguish, chaos, and loneliness from which one and the other spring, so that what I'd like to tell him is *I understand you perfectly*—must nevertheless accept that my immediate rejection of his piteous assertion, *I should have stayed with my family*, be taken as a formal statement of compassion.

I also have words of praise for his work, and I tell him, with conviction, that others would declare themselves satisfied if they had accomplished as much.

But nothing helps.

It seems it isn't always a good thing to make him talk.

Or he isn't in the mood.

Then, if it's impossible to go out, I force him to watch a movie (nothing dark; classic comedies by Lubitsch or Howard Hawks), and more and more often we listen to music, albums that he asks me to buy: Dylan's *Modern Times*, Tom Waits's *Orphans*, JJ Cale and Eric Clapton's *Road to Escondido*, a Georges Brassens collection, an old Leonard Cohen album, another by Portabales, which have the virtue of lifting his spirits.

Every day, too, we repeat the same nighttime routine. I help him into bed, arrange on his bedside table everything he might need if he wakes in the middle of the night, and sit for a while at the foot of his bed . . . When at last I go up to the apartment where my wife and I sleep, I call him briefly on his cell phone to check that the monitor is working, and no matter what kind of day it's been, he whimpers for a few seconds, pretending to cry like a baby. Sometimes—rarely—after that heroic display of humor, I leave the monitor in the care of my wife and escape to a bar to meet some friend. What never changes is our morning ritual, which follows the same pattern as the nighttime one: a pretend whimper before he says good morning and rouses himself.

Meanwhile, just before Christmas, his oncologist tells us that he's very weak and that he should try a break from the treatment, and later, taking me aside, she explains that the chemotherapy isn't working and it won't be administered to him again. I should prepare for an end that won't be long in coming, she warns. At first she's reluctant to give me a time frame, but finally she allows that it might be a month, three at most.

Thanks to a friend, I've found a doctor willing to honor the wishes expressed in my father's living will. If before I had no doubts about what I'm preparing to do, I have even fewer when I learn from the doctor the many painful forms—depending on which organ fails first—in which something as apparently simple as death can present itself. After he tells me what symptoms to watch for so that I'll be ready, I leave the office with a strange sense of duty done, which automatically rusts over with grief when I get home and face my father's gaze.

The Christmas celebrations are a prolongation rather than an interruption; a confirmation, not a departure. We spend the night of the twenty-fourth in Madrid with his family. He's happy, has a few drinks, and though no one treats him with special deference and things are lively with all the children around, I can see in people's expressions and their manner the same sense of anticipated mourning that has come over me. Days later we go to Galicia with my mother and my wife. Before we board the plane, he tries to convince us to change our minds, with the argument that he's just been there, but in the end he seems to enjoy the trip. He takes pleasure in the house, our drives, any distraction. One day when he's alone, he slips as he's hurrying to answer his cell phone. He cuts himself and can't get up. I still have the gauze and disinfectant that I used to tend to him. One day he buys a vacuum cleaner. Another day he paints greenish gray the frame of a Renaissance panel painting belonging to my mother. The night of the thirty-first, as the year is rung out, he sits in a chair and I stand next to him. We both know that we'll toast each other first and wait until later to toast the others, but a certain amount of time—a very long time, it seems to me—passes before we do, and during that time we stare at each other. His eyes are very open and fixed on mine, and though I force myself to smile, I can't keep it up as long as he can. How to wish someone a happy new year when he won't have one? His gaze doesn't flag, but mine slips away for an instant as I bend toward him, tapping his glass with mine, wishing him a happy new year, and giving him a kiss as I try to smile. His is the distorted gaze of a sick man, which is why it's hard to interpret; I don't know whether what he seeks in my face is the vision of a future that's still unknowable, or whether it's the next step: the recognition of his fate and an acquiescent desire to comfort, to feel and elicit feeling, to give what will soon be impossible for him to give.

In January, back in Madrid, everything happens with deceptive slowness. I look for a home health aide; I teach the doctors who begin to visit us not to treat him like someone terminally ill; I keep careful track of the passing days and his strength in order to decide when to give him the cortisone that will grant him a ten-day grace period; I call his oncologist in order to carry on a simulated conversation in his presence that makes him believe that all is not lost, that he'll restart the treatment when he's stronger; I get someone he trusts to ask him whether he'd like to see the friend he met in Brazil, not wanting him to be left with that wish, if he has it; I gather photographs and biographical material and write the draft of an obituary to send to the newspapers when the moment comes; I buy a hospital bed, which, in addition to making his life easier now that he spends so much time lying down, is intended as false proof that the end isn't so near; and meanwhile, I continue to oversee the renovation work on the apartment where we'll supposedly live, the completion of which he pleads with me for, asking with growing insistence whether I think he'll see it finished, whether I think he'll ever live there.

I remember one sunny morning when we go out for a walk with my mother and visit the San Isidro Museum; I remember another morning, this time with my wife, when we have breakfast on the Plaza Mayor and then try to go to FNAC to buy music; I remember a lunch at my aunt's house; I remember pirated DVDs of *Marie Antoinette*, *Little Miss Sunshine*, and *The Queen*; I remember friends coming to say goodbye; I remember the visit of two young artists, women, who—not by chance, I believe—my father greets with Tom Waits, the most jarringly discordant of all the albums in our scanty collection at the pseudo-duplex; I remember a day when we have lunch at a Chinese restaurant and afterward go to visit a photographer friend, and as we drink whiskey and listen to an old Slim Gaillard and Slam Stewart jam session, the friend takes twenty shots of us with a Leica; I remember one day when he surprises me by asking me to buy paper and watercolors; I remember one morning when I give him a new appointment book and he fills out the first page in shaky handwriting, giving the address of the building where it was now almost certain that he would never live; I remember a tea that I prepare, according to his instructions, for three of his female cousins; I remember a friend, someone he hasn't seen in a while, who brings him two CDs of Mozambican music from the seventies; I remember his praise for his new bed; I remember the first time he doesn't get up until noon; I remember one morning when I come down from the apartment where my wife and I sleep to find him collapsed on the bathroom floor, unable to get up; I remember his look of mute assent when I tell him that from now on, I'll sleep in the apartment with him, on a mattress on the floor; I remember the nights when, if he needs to go to the bathroom, he rings a little bell to call me and I assist him in his fragile walk; I remember the extreme care with which he listens to everything I tell him regarding his condition; I remember his growing detachment from the reality that surrounds him, his lack of interest in anything to do with his past struggles; I remember his weary words after the visit of two disciples who come to see him on one of his last days and talk to him about painting, thinking to entertain him; I remember the drop of blood that falls on one of my shoes when I bandage a scrape for him. I'm wearing them now; the reddish ring is still visible.

My father died in February. By December we knew what was coming. He, apparently, let himself be deceived. At the end of January, he experienced a fleeting revival thanks to the cortisone, and when this wore off like the illusion it was, he attributed his rapid weakening to the belated effects of the last chemotherapy session. He repeated this to everyone who came to see him. Especially the doctors who made house calls. Polite and formal until the end, he begged their pardon for being unable to get up, for making them come to him. I called the angels of death one Saturday when he began to speak incoherently, and on Sunday morning a doctor and a nurse came. They were with us for four hours, during which they gave him the first dose of drugs (an opiate, and a derivative of lysergic acid to combat the nightmares) and showed me how to give him further doses as needed, until in two or three days the end came. They left us prepared to expect a wait, but as so often over the course of his illness, there was no wait. My father died that same night. He died alone, in his room, while in the living room my mother and my wife tried to convince me to go in to him, since—as indeed happened—he might die that very night. I refused because it had been an especially hectic day, with multiple visitors in addition to the doctor and nurse, and I wanted to let him rest, and also because we'd had the same argument the night before and I felt bolstered by the precedent. Though his death loomed over us, and at moments I wished for it, I refused to contemplate it. I won the argument, as I had won it the night before, and when my wife and I went into his room half an hour later, this time with the practical purpose of turning him in bed, my father was gone. That's the main thing I remember. The feeling that he had gone. Of course there were tears, scattered words, hurried searches for a mirror, tremendous anxiety, and at last, when we had accepted that he was dead, I embraced him and began to talk to him as if he could still hear me. And yet in all that time, ever since I had come into the room, I never lost the feeling—the painful feeling, because it was a physical absence—that my father was gone. The body that lay in the bed and that I was embracing was no longer my father. My father had vanished, had gone to nowhere, the place where memory is defeated and disappears. For the first and only time in my life, my hopeful agnosticism gave way to the harshness of atheism.

Two hours later I helped a nurse prepare his body for burial. Ten hours later I was heading into one of the big department stores to buy the outfit that I would wear at the wake. Twelve hours later I was calling the art critics at the three big national papers to give them the news and ask them to write his obituary. Two days later I received the urn with his ashes, and I buried it, at his sister's request, where his parents lay. Four days later, on my own, I got rid of most of his clothes. Three weeks later I emptied his apartment. A month later I moved his paintings to a new storage space out of fear that the friend he met in Brazil would try to seize them. Two months later the work on my mother's old apartment was finished, the place where my wife and I were supposed to live with him. The day of the move, I gave away the ergonomic chair he had used during most of his illness. Three months later, on a terrace at the Círculo de Bellas Artes in Madrid, I hosted a cocktail reception with jazz, the party he had requested as a lay funeral. While I was organizing it, I couldn't help thinking that he would have been horrified at the expense, but—always unsure of my affections—he wouldn't have been unmoved by this public display of filial loyalty. Four months later I retrieved his last paintings from the studio of the artist friend who had been keeping them since September, leaving behind his easel, a chest of drawers, two chairs, a big basket for papers, and a table. I spent an afternoon choosing what to get rid of, what to keep, what to give away. Five months later I went on vacation. Seven months later I got rid of his glasses. I threw them, along with his last bag, into a Dumpster.

This is the first thing I wrote when I could write:

It's been eight months since my father died and two years since we learned that he was sick. In all this time I've hardly written a thing. I didn't have the time or the head for it. I haven't read, either. I've lived facing outward, split into as many facets and tasks as his needs demanded. I've been his main companion, his intermediary with the doctors, his psychologist, his helper, his executive arm, his waiter and nurse. I've set my own life aside, annulled myself, and merged with him. I've been his partner, the person who accompanied him to the hospital on chemotherapy days, who stayed with him while the treatment was administered, who took him home, who answered his questions, who supplied the strategies of deceit calculated to nourish hope and who consoled him when hope was elusive, who encouraged him to make the decisions that only he could make and who began to make them for him when he couldn't make them. It was I who designed the approach to his future and set it in motion, making sure that each element, each thing that I did or suggested, seemed normal and not dictated by his impending death. I've measured my words, I've made jokes when I didn't feel like it, I've lied, I've held my tongue, and I've meted out my silences when the vagaries of his married life advised it. I've gone to live with him, done the shopping for him, cooked; I've spent all day on the phone trying to get information, dealing with bureaucracy, asking for help, giving detailed accounts of his condition to everyone who called. I've signed papers, I've talked to notaries and lawyers, I've secured the money from the sale of the house that he shared with his wife, I've made transfers, rented safe-deposit boxes, and negotiated with bank employees. I've transported furniture and paintings, I've rented storage spaces to keep them in, I've been builder and architect of the house where we were going to live, as well as of the little studio where he was supposedly going to paint as long as illness permitted, but most of all I've lived for him, only him. I've had no other occupation. I've learned to watch him, to be alert to his changing symptoms in order to anticipate the different ends that his many metastases left unknown, consulting with doctors, planning the exact time to step in (neither too soon nor too late, as he asked me to do when he learned he was sick, though he didn't want to know too much about it). I've visited pharmacies and clinics almost daily, I've taken care of unexpected cuts and scrapes, I've helped him in and out of bed, I've led him to and from the bathroom, I've feared his death, I've wished for it at moments, and when all that was left was suffering and no joy that the pain didn't cancel out, I made the call that he asked me to make. I received the doctors who this time weren't coming to heal him, I let them teach me what to do, I waited for his death, I saw him die, and I dressed him in his burial clothes. I've carried out his wishes in every possible way, and the effort of it has left me exhausted. Exhausted and empty.

I never thought it would be so simple. I always imagined that it would be more tortuous, that the skein we had patiently wound between us wouldn't vanish with him.

Then come all the failed attempts that I talked about at the beginning.

I've included parts from some of them in this book.

And all the reading about fathers and mothers and mourning that I talked about too.

But I wasn't constant.

For a long time I was lost, and I let time go by. I did things I shouldn't have done.

I had money. My father's money. A cushion of sorts.

And I amused myself.

I went out, I stayed out late, I went to the movies, I had dinner and lunch out, and I spent hours each day finishing the apartment where my father would never live with my wife and me, putting up bookcases, arranging furniture, upholstering sofas, decorating it as he would have done. Better, in one regard: I didn't economize. I also hung more paintings of his than he would have hung.

I saw people I hadn't seen for a while and I learned to tell them what had happened to me. The short version for those who simply asked, the longer and more detailed one for those who wanted more, and, for special occasions, the one explaining how his wishes were carried out. It was in these trial efforts that I began to use the image of the circle.

One day the newspaper I write for asked me to review a book. Little by little I began to lead a life resembling the one I'd had before my father got sick, and another day, in the early stages of the writing of this memoir, I wrote the first chapter almost in one sitting.

Since then, there've been many times when I wanted to give it up, and each crisis was followed by periods of straying.

My scruples only grew, as did the fear of hurting others, and my doubts about whether what I was writing would transcend the interest it held for me and take on literary substance.

But no matter how long I strayed, I always came back to it in the end.

Partly out of stubbornness, partly because I felt that it couldn't be any other way, partly because I lacked the energy to quit a book and start from nothing again.

And especially, I suppose, because I didn't want to abandon my father so soon.

As a result, I've written and I've run, I've written and I've run; and no matter which it was, the only way I went was around in circles.

Meanwhile I've kept reading. Modiano: *Un pedigree*; Pamuk: *My Father's Suitcase*; Simenon: *Letter to My Mother*; Héctor Abad: *Oblivion*; Peter Handke: *A Sorrow Beyond Dreams*; Juan Cruz Ruiz: *Ojalá octubre*; Simone de Beauvoir: *A Very Easy Death*; Giani Stuparich: *L'Isola*; Lolita Bosch: *La familia de mi padre*; A. M. Homes: *The Mistress's Daughter*; J.M.G. Le Clézio: *The African*.

And from the opposite perspective, the father's: *Quieto* by Màrius Serra; *Wrong About Japan* by Peter Carey; *The Film Club* by David Gilmour . . .

I read a graphic novel about a father and his autistic daughter.

And though it isn't directly related to the father-son pairing, Perec's *Je me souviens.*

Circles. Random but always suggestive books, like *My Life as a Russian Novel* by Emmanuel Carrère.

Or essays, like María Zambrano's on confession as a literary genre.

And I recently saw a documentary film: *My Architect* by Nathaniel Kahn, in which Kahn follows the trail of his father, the American architect Louis Kahn, whom he hardly knew.

In the film, Louis Kahn says something obvious that nevertheless made me think: "How accidental we are, our existences are, really, and how full of influence by circumstance." He's referring to his decision to become an architect, and I can't say whether his son, the director of the documentary, meant to lend added meaning to the statement by using it to conclude two segments, but the fact is that it can easily be extrapolated to fit the more personal subject of his film: the complex ties that bind us to our origins, the need to make peace with them. In essence, our life is composed of fortuitous events. Infinite possibilities spring from each decision we make, not to mention the effects of others' decisions on us. The future is uncertain; we live in the present. The past is the only thing that seems fixed, and we tend to mythicize it. It gives us something to rebel against or reconcile with. Parents may or may not serve the same purpose, and for that reason alone they are sources of conflict. At the very least, they're guilty of having brought us into the world.

Nursing a wound might be profitable from an artistic standpoint. But only the strongest of us or those who've been gravely injured can live forever with an open wound.

Besides, and this quickly becomes clear, our predecessors

were also creatures of fate, also had scores to settle, were also cheated.

Each of us is just one more piece in a child's Meccano set, and we matter only as much as we come to believe that we matter.

All the books I've been reading, no matter what drives them, whether it be filial devotion, the urge for revenge, remorse, or mere literary ambition, simply confirm this fact.

Our troubles aren't exclusive to us. To a greater or lesser degree and in one way or another, everyone has faced them.

And most of us, at one point or another, have wanted to resolve them once and for all.

Close the circle.

Though some—just a few—do it only to say yet again: I was right.

And to make a record of it.

For someone of my grandfather's generation, success as a father meant dealing his children a hand no worse than the one he'd been dealt. Beginning with my father's generation, it hasn't been so easy, maybe because we've gotten softer. For further confirmation, we have the testimony of Sibylle Lacan's *Un père*.

My father didn't squander the poor hand that he was dealt. He bettered it. He amounted to more than his father ever did. He was a cultured and sensitive man. Curious about almost everything.

And unlike my grandfather, who was the very image of failure, he didn't fail.

Though it wasn't enough for him, though in the end he didn't get all the recognition he deserved, he was an excellent painter. He never conspired against others, never shut anyone out, as others had done to him.

He liked his work. Toward the end he lived almost exclusively for art. For looking at art, thinking about art, making art.

That much he had. No matter what he said at the end, in the cold fever of approaching death. Unlike my grandfather, his father, who spent his life seeking success in business and was left with nothing when all his ventures failed.

The friend he met in Brazil counts as a failure, impossible to deny it. And yet it would be unfair for him to make his entrance into the next world with that mark against him. No one who gives generously and is betrayed nonetheless, no one who takes a blow when he's down and doesn't shed a tear, can be said to have failed.

Did my father and my grandfather ever talk? Did they make peace with each other?

I don't think so.

And yet I'm sure that my father forgave him. That what he minded most, in any case, was never having told him what all parents want to hear on their children's lips at least once: your mistakes don't count, your intentions were good, and time simply got the better of you.

Because at the end of the day, that's our greatest mistake, from which all others spring: we think that time is much more forgiving than it is.

And that there's time for everything, when in fact there isn't.

I had the time to tell this to my father—not just tell him, but show him—and he did everything he could to smooth the way. There are no scores to be settled; there were none when I began to write.

And, of course, no guilt about his death for which I might seek forgiveness. So strong is my sense of having done right that I haven't even resorted to the exculpatory urge to tell myself that he died of natural causes, since the drugs the doctors gave him, which I was taught to administer, weren't supposed to take effect so soon.

And no guilt, of course, for having tried to deceive him about his illness.

And none for the departure of the friend he met in Brazil.

And none for being unable to say whether my behavior would have been impeccable if his life had been longer. My cards were marked—I knew he was going to die—but so were his.

Both of us tried. A year and a half of our lives we gave each other.

It's not fair, then, to torment myself about what might have been. It simply was.

That, too, I owe to him.

The only real guilt that occasionally nags at me: having delayed, having let time nearly get the better of us. And my excess of zeal.

Nothing substantial enough, in any case, to feed all the pages I've written.

Having realized this and being able to express it is perhaps the one thing I've gained.

In this regard, writing time and living time coincide.

Would I have come to the same conclusion if I hadn't written it?

Getting used to his death. That's the main thing I've done in all this time.

Death. That which cannot be thought, it's said.

From the day of his death to the day on which I write this, March 24, 2009, I've seen—to the best of my recollection—a Miguel Ángel Campano show, I've seen an Albert Oehlen show (both painters he respected), I've seen a Kippenberger show, I've seen a Darío Villalba show, I've seen a Dürer show, I've seen a Patinir show; I've seen a show titled *The Abstraction of Landscape*, I've seen a Joseph Beuys show, I've seen a show of Javier Riera's photographs, I've seen an Alejandro Corujeira show, I've seen a Julio Zachrisson show, I've seen a show of avant-garde movements in the time of art historian Carl Einstein, I've seen a Nancy Spero show, I've seen a show of Greco-Roman sculpture, I've seen a show of Renaissance portraits, I've seen a Picasso show, I've seen a Tàpies show, I've seen a Rembrandt show, I've seen a Twombly show, I've seen a show of the work of a Spanish photographer whose name I can't recall, I've seen a Juan Ugalde show, I've seen shows in the same gallery by Bendix Harms, a young German I liked, and by Secundino Hernández, whom I'd never heard of, I've seen a strident show of contemporary Chinese artists, I've seen a show by the Czech photographer Sudek, and the other day, on my way back from doing the shopping, I went into a gallery because I thought I glimpsed a distant resemblance to my father's final works in the way that space was sliced up in the paintings in the window. Cristina Lama, born in 1977 in Sevilla, was the artist.

And I'm forgetting a few, I suppose. Shows that I saw accompanied by his ghost, as it were.

Many days spent without hearing a person's voice on the phone are needed to understand his absence; many days spent resisting the impulse to call are needed to understand that he'll no longer answer; many days spent silencing remarks meant only for him are needed to understand that this is how it will be from now on; many days spent wondering what he'd say about something that we're well aware he knew best are needed to understand that now our own judgment will have to suffice; many days spent looking at pictures of him are needed to understand that these are pictures of a dead person; many days spent contemplating the objects we inherited are needed to understand that they're no longer his but ours; many days spent taking stock of common experiences are needed to understand that they'll never be repeated, that all that's left of them is the memory. A memory, too, that won't remain unchanged.

I've been down that road. I've caught myself thinking about calling my father when he'd been dead for months; I've found consolation in gazing at things that were his and then felt the desire to avoid looking at them as my eye grew accustomed to them and made them mine; I've saved up questions for the next time I'd see him without realizing that it would never come.

A month ago, going to see a show that I was asked to write about, I felt freed for the first time of his ghost. I was in a hurry, working on deadline, and I hardly thought of him until the next morning, when I saw the article in print and wanted his approval, as I always used to when I wrote about art.

Days later, at a Bacon retrospective, he was on my mind; I couldn't stop thinking about him. He made the rounds with me, prodding me to reject psychological interpretations and just look at the painting, but it wasn't enough. I felt a little lost. I needed his commentary, which, though always admiring, wouldn't have failed to alert me to Bacon's every slip, every mannerist flaw.

Life doesn't stop.

Seven months ago, early in September 2008, I learned that I would be a father at the end of the following May. Just a month and a half from now.

Life doesn't stop. Life has gradually carried me away from him, mitigating his absence. Not the pain, which—though buried deep—is surely the same as it was when I began to write. The same as it will always be. As I write this, with a Django Reinhardt album of his playing in the background, I know with cruel clarity that he is no longer painting in his studio, as I so often imagined him. His studio doesn't exist, his paintings are in storage, and the next show of his work, if I can manage it, will be a retrospective.

Life doesn't stop. I'm coming to the end of this book.

If I could turn back the clock and change the way I was for so many years, I would do it, but to say so now, when I already know the ending—even if I mean it—is false tender.

So I think about my unborn son, who will bear his name, and I ask myself how I'll mold him, how I'll fail him, what I'll have to forgive him for, and what he'll have to forgive me for when—if he doesn't do it sooner—I, like my father, fade into nothingness.

What he'll remember fondly about me.

I'd like to preseve some of the best of my father so that it passes on to him through me.

Madrid, April 16, 2009

A Note About the Author

Marcos Giralt Torrente was born in Madrid in 1968 and is the author of three novels, a novella, and a book of short stories. He was a writer in residence at the Royal Spanish Academy in Rome and at the University of Aberdeen, and was part of the Berlin Artists-in-Residence Program in 2002–2003. He is the recipient of several distinguished awards, including the Spanish National Book Award in 2011. His works have been translated into French, German, Greek, Italian, Korean, and Portuguese.

A Note About the Translator

Natasha Wimmer has translated Roberto Bolaño's *2666*, for which she was awarded the PEN Translation prize in 2009, and *The Savage Detectives*, among many other works. She lives in New York City.